PICTURE THIS

A Gallery of Fusible Appliqué
Projects for Quilting and Framing

Jean Wells & Marina Anderson

Copyright © 1990 Jean Wells

Front cover photo:
Star Bright

Back cover photos:
Old-fashioned Santa
Wedding Heart
Bears and Bow Ties Nap Pillow

Photography by Indivar Sivanathan
Bend, Oregon

Picture framing by Paul Nichamoff
Frame Attic
Sisters, Oregon

Editing by Nadene M. Hartley
Copy editing by Sayre Van Young

Design and typesetting by Virginia Coull
C&T Publishing

Illustrations by Marina Anderson
Bend, Oregon

Published by
C&T Publishing
P.O. Box 1456
Lafayette, CA 94549

ISBN: 0-914881-31-0

All rights reserved. No part of this work covered by the copyright hereon may be reproduced or used in any form or by any means— graphic, electronic, or mechanical, including photocopying, recording, taping, or information storage and retrieval systems, without written permission of the publisher.

Library of Congress Catalog Card No.: 90-62259

Printed in the United States of America

Table of Contents

Friendship in Gift Giving 5

Giving Thoughts 7
    From Marina 7
    From Jean 8

The Basics 9
    The Color Palette 10
    Background Fabric 10
    Appliqué Fabrics 11
    Trimming 11
    Necessities 11
    Construction 12
    Machine Appliqué 15
    Dimensional Fusing 16
    Borders and Bindings 16
    Quilting 16
    Pillows 17
    Framing and Finishing 17

Picture This 19
    1. The Friendship Fan 19
    2. Quilter's Garden 20
    3. Evening Quilter's Garden 20
    4. Oriental Fan 25
    5. Crazy Patch Heart 25
    6. Heavenly Angel 26
    7. Old-fashioned Santa 27
    8. Christmas Tree 27
    9. Celestial Angel 28
    10. Corner Fan 29
    11. Tulip Fan 30
    12. Pastel House and Heart 30
    13. Victorian Santa 31
    14. Country House and Heart ... 31
    15. Layered Hearts
        A. Wedding Heart 32
        B. Valentine Heart 32
    16. Bordered Fan 41
    17. Bunny Kisses Quilt 42
    18. Bunny Kisses Pillow 44
    19. Bears and Bow Ties Quilt 45
    20. Bears and Bow Ties Nap Pillow 47
    21. Star Bright 48

Wrapping It Up 49
    Gift Tags 50

About the Authors 51

Patterns 52

Color photographs on pages 21-24 and 33-40

Friendship in Gift Giving

Grandma always said, "It means more when you make it!" A great portion of her life was spent always giving a little of herself through her handwork. Many of us grew up with that "giving seed" planted in our memory. When heart is directing hand, we create with a special magic.

The "picture" projects shown throughout this book are perfect for giving. They are fashioned of fabrics, laces, and trims that are fused, glued, and stitched to create a simple and straightforward gift. But within the framework of fabric or wood, hangs a visible, lasting symbol of caring sentiments from maker to recipient.

Some of the projects here are perfect for the obvious seasonal times of giving, such as Christmas, Valentine's Day, or Easter. But give thought also to the "seasons of the heart"—telling a friend how special she is, a baby's birth, welcome to a new home, or a naptime pillow for that special little boy. These fabric pictures truly create memories of the heart.

In this collection of heartfelt pictures, we've also included pillows (sofa "pictures") and a couple of crib quilts (baby "pictures"). Some things just need to be plumped rather than hung! Several of the designs are quilted, some embellished, some neither. For most of the projects, you will be able to decide just how much detail (and time) you want to add. We include some basic framing instructions so you can choose to frame your picture yourself, if you'd like. To complete the package, coordinating reproducible gift tags have been designed to complement your pictures.

Our gift to you is cover-to-cover innovative techniques and a full variety of designs in which you can give of heart and hand.

Giving Thoughts

From Marina

Pictures, pictures, I've always loved to do pictures. As a child if I wasn't drawing, I was coloring, if not coloring, then painting.... Doing a special picture for someone was my way of expressing feelings. The chronological history of my work hangs not in my studio, but in the homes of dear family and friends (some of the more primitive pieces I'm sure occupy drawers and boxes). I've always found it difficult to explain why I didn't keep my most special pieces until I started working on this book. As Jean and I discussed motivation to create, it became clear. I keep the joy in my heart, the love and the memories that it took to produce that special gift of art.

My discovery of the fusing technique came about in a rather humorous way. Deep into the shadows of the deadline of our previous book, *A Celebration of Hearts*, it became evident that I was going to have to dust off my machine and sew. Primarily I use my time for my expertise...design, color, and concepts. I feared my license to sew had expired! As fate would have it, I never got the opportunity to get behind the wheel, as I discovered my machine was stuck in reverse. With time as a key element, fusing found its way into my life.

My first venture was the "Crazy at Heart" picture from *Hearts*. As I moved from one step to the next, my excitement grew. With completion within a matter of hours (frame and all), I was elated! And the completed project passed my most critical test... I hung it on the wall, stood back and said, "I'd buy it!"

Giving of heart and hand should not dictate quantity of time spent in the making. That is the exciting surprise element in *Picture This*. You can create with fabric and trims and choose your personal level of time involvement.

The procedure itself begins with a good design, simple yet incorporating areas of visual interest. Next, playtime with the fabrics: prints, color, and texture all working together. Finally, the trimming. This is a relaxing, almost therapeutic procedure. For those of you who have avoided fusing—"From scratch is always better"—I have a small secret to share. I recently confessed to my mother-in-law that last year I accidentally left the giblets in the holiday turkey (paper and all). She sort of gasped and rolled her eyes, but *I* knew the stuffing was great. Sometimes, it doesn't matter how you get there if the end results are good!

You may wonder why Jean and I chose a gift theme for this book. Why not just a plain follow-the-directions-get-it-done-and-who-cares-what-you-do-with-it book? It might have been simpler, but it felt closer to our feelings about the importance of giving—on many levels—to do it this way. A personal experience illustrating a giving of heart comes to mind.

I moved to Bend, Oregon, quite recently, a happy

move since Jean and I were finally within a short drive, but sad in that I left behind a dear friend, Carrie. When I left, I gave her the "Forever Friends" fused and framed picture done for the *Hearts* book. In parting, we cried and hugged, then sadly went on to our separate lives miles apart. In September, Carrie decided to return to college. Having been away from a classroom for years, she found a college-level English assignment indeed a frightening thing. Specifically, she was to write about something in her life that meant a lot to her. Carrie chose to tell about the picture I had given to her. Let me share her closing paragraph with you.

"Now, when our family gathers at dinner and we talk about our day, her picture sits above us, watching over us and letting me know how important it has become to have best friends forever." She got an A.

From Jean

One of the most gratifying parts of my work in fabric arts is sharing a new idea with my students. When Marina first showed me the fused crazy heart, I loved the look of it! My second reaction was a surprised, "It doesn't even look fused!" To me, a former home economics teacher trained in the 60s, fusing was a dirty word. Then all the possibilities started popping into my mind. I knew this was destined to be a class act—in other words, "My students will love it!"

Prior to the first class, I made half a dozen or so fused crazy hearts in varying color combinations to inspire my students. I was amazed! Each heart took on such an individual look just by differing the colors and trims. The day of the class arrived and the students began to file in. They were eager, but I sensed a bit of skepticism (in the past we had all wrinkled our noses at fusing). Three short hours later, as they departed with a completed project in hand, the vote was unanimous—this definitely wasn't cheating. Instead, it opened up a new avenue of creating: not only a new outlet for fabric, color, and design, but also an opportunity to be creative with time. We so often feel the desire to make beautiful things, but busy lives sometimes limit what we can commit to. Why deny yourself the satisfaction of completion when fusible art can fill that need?

Being a quilter at heart, it wasn't long before quilting crept into the design process in a big way. My projects just seem to end up quilts whether free hanging or framed. But that's one of the wonderful things about these projects: you can quilt, or not. You can embellish, or not.... The possibilities and variations are unlimited.

These projects are great confidence builders. Pictures give you an opportunity to work with putting fabrics together and to dabble with embellishment tricks and techniques. And why are these projects so easy?

It's the repetition of a few simple steps that will perfect the process. To be successful however, you do need to follow certain color and design guidelines. But more about that later in the book.

Any and all of our designs can be enlarged or reduced on a copy machine to fit a favorite frame or wall space. Some of the designs I have chosen to appliqué, as you can see on the children's quilts. They can all be quilted. Let your own skills and capabilities lead you in directions other than the ones we have suggested.

Marina and I come to you with varying experiences. By pooling our talents and ideas, we bring you our very best. Do enjoy *Picture This: A Gallery of Fusible Appliqué Projects for Quilting and Framing.*

Teaching Hints

Any of these projects would be great for a hands-on class experience. As the instructor, plan on bringing some of the general tools needed. Having the necessities makes these fun projects even simpler and easier. Further, bringing some extra scraps from your scrap collection will also help those students who are a little bored with their own current collections. Plus, it's a nice way to share....

For information about the authors' other books and a free catalog of C&T quilting books, write to:

C&T Publishing
P.O. Box 1456
Lafayette, CA 94549

The Basics

Picture This is a book of many faces. Any of the designs can be professionally framed, framed by you, quilted and mounted on a rod, or made into a pillow. The possibilities are endless. There are several ways to proceed on a project.

For example, you can create your picture leaving plenty of background fabric and decide the finishing later. In this way, your ideas will develop as you go. Allowing plenty of background fabric means borders can be added or excess fabric can be trimmed off to fit a frame. Or you can begin by choosing a design to fit a favorite frame. Make sure the nature of the design is in keeping with the style of frame. Then fabric choices should echo that theme. The frame sets the parameters of the design choices. Sometimes, special occasions or particular places in the home might dictate the design selected. Always follow through on a theme or mood once the decision is made.

If you decide to make a picture for a wall, trims can be glued in place. If the picture is to become a pillow (a sofa "picture"), trims should be stitched in place. Consider whether the picture will be laundered on a regular basis. The baby quilts in this book can easily be wall pictures, but most likely will end up in the crib keeping baby warm. So we opted to machine appliqué those projects for sturdiness.

The copy machine will become your friend as you devise ways to use pictures. All of the patterns were made to fit the page size of this book. Each set of project instructions tells you if the design needs to be enlarged or reduced, and gives the percentage setting for the copy machine. Reducing and enlarging on a copy machine can boggle some of the most creative minds. To simplify for all, we just give the size percentage setting. Once you're actually standing at the copy machine, it will make sense, but if the machine still seems a bit intimidating (they all work differently), have an attendant set it up for you.

To best use this book, first read through this section on "The Basics." All the general information that will make these projects a success for you is covered here. Consider it your classroom time. These hints and techniques will not only make your experience more successful, but more fun. Though these are "spontaneous" projects—and even though you are working with fabric scraps and making decisions as you go along—a good grounding in "the basics" will make your final result far more rewarding.

A list of necessities—materials needed for picture construction and for framing—is included. You probably won't need them all for any one project, but having these items around will mean you won't have to stop in the middle of a project to hunt that needed tool.

To avoid repetition, the general instructions for appliqué, trimming, constructing, binding, quilting, and framing are given in "The Basics" and are not repeated for each project. Any variations or additions, however, are noted.

Then, as you move to the section "Picture This," it's time to choose a specific project. Each project description relates not only to the detailing of the design, but also to possible gift-giving ideas. The materials lists suggest a good supply base to work from in making your picture. You may—or may not—need everything in each list. Since most pictures are made from scraps, having a full range of items available makes it easier and less confusing to substitute. Always refer to the photographs while making fabric and trim decisions. When we work, we gather a variety of trims that might work and spread them on the table, choosing placement as we go along. Consider the detailed list of materials more a frame of reference than a list of absolutes. "Wrapping It Up" is just that. Gift tags are provided for you to reproduce, to add that final—and special—touch to your gifts.

This book is our gift to you to enjoy.

The Color Palette

The finished appeal of your appliquéd picture will result from careful choice of colors in both fabric and trims. From experience, we've learned that too much contrast results in a very spotty look. Remember, these are small pictures and the eye needs to feel continuity. One of my first pictures used half red fabric and half green fabric, and it just didn't work. I think the eye just couldn't decide if it was a green picture or a red one. The color plan needs to be "mostly something with an accent." The mostly something part can be different shades and textures. Try to be sure that the color plan has a color theme throughout. A palette can be as subtle as creams and whites with a soft peach accent or as bright as holiday reds with a sprinkling of green. As you sort through your scraps, pick anything that's in the mood of the fabrics that might work. Most of the time scraps will work, but sometimes you need a larger piece for a wing or panel. Refer to the photographs often. They're meant to be a frame of reference, both for design and color selection.

Since the emphasis of these projects is on wall art, take into account where your completed project is destined to go. Consider not only the color cues of a room but also its style and mood. Though it isn't necessary to perfectly match room colors—in fact that can be very boring—do make sure the fabrics have a compatible mood with the room.

Pictures make wonderful gifts and also can be made seasonal by choices of appropriate holiday fabrics. Our angel was first done in whites, silvers, and golds for the holiday season. Then we decided to make her up in a Victorian mood. She could also be done to match a little girl's bedroom. Let your imagination be your guide.

Background Fabric

Before you begin, think about all the components of your project. There is the background fabric, scraps of fabric for the appliqué, sometimes a border, and trimmings. Each of these has to be appealing on its own, be compatible with the others, and harmonize with the area where the finished project will be placed. Quite a balancing act!

The background should provide a pleasing backdrop for the appliqué fabrics. A light-colored background appears airy, fresh, and bright, while a dark background seems more dramatic. Of course, a medium background presents the biggest challenge. When selecting the appliqué fabrics to put on a medium background, contrast is important. Most of the time, choosing a totally different color will achieve the needed contrast. Look at the angel in Photo 9; her background is a dark blue and the appliqué fabrics are in shades of maroons and teals. This combination really does work, but it involved careful planning and much trial-and-error fabric selection.

The background fabric can be a print, but use a subtle one that doesn't fight with the variety of appliqué fabrics. A print background appears as a texture when viewed from a distance. If you choose a floral background, your appliqué choices could be all solids or subtle prints. Make sure the print can't be seen through any of the solids. (That's one of those things—if you don't carefully check at the beginning—that can sneak up and surprise you at the end. Not a happy discovery.) Study the choices we've made for fabrics. Don't go out and try to find the same fabric, but do keep in mind the types of fabrics and colors we've chosen, and how we've combined them.

Appliqué Fabrics

After you've settled on your background fabric, choosing the appliqué fabrics is your next challenge. A suggestion: observe where we've used a darker fabric versus a lighter one and apply that general principle to your own color palette. Notice that some of our choices have a subtle change of design from fabric to fabric whereas others have a more direct change. An example is the two Santas—first in traditional reds, green, and gold accents (Photo 7). Now look at the Santa in Photo 13, featuring an upholstery stripe background in roses and grays with gold accents. This second Santa has a Victorian flair while the other is more old-fashioned and "country"-looking. We used exactly the same design, but with very different color palettes.

Only small pieces of fabrics, with a few larger ones for wings or panels, are needed for the projects, so your scrap fabric collection will be put to good use. Don't forget taffetas, satins, velveteens, linens, decorator fabrics, and old laces. A change in texture can add special interest to the finished picture. Look again at the Victorian Santa (Photo 13) and see the variety of fabrics used.

We have even had students come to class with a large print and use only that in their appliqué. The pieces for the appliqué were cut from different sections of the fabric where there were color changes. Then the trims were added at the end to give sparkle. Look closely at your own fabrics. Sometimes there's a part of a larger design that will work perfectly (and unexpectedly) in one of these projects—perhaps a bouquet of roses that can be isolated and featured in an interesting spot. Your fabric can give you inspiration. Let it.

When you are satisfied with the fabrics you've selected, pile them up on a table. Walk away. Turn around and take a quick glance at them. Does the combination settle right in your mind? You will know at a glance if a fabric isn't working in the group. It will jump out at you. If it jumps out at you on the table, it will do the same in the final picture. Sometimes just using a little less of the fabric will take care of the problem. Or, if it was your favorite, find new companions for it. It's just that simple!

Trimming

Trimming choices are the icing on the cake. They should be in keeping theme-wise with the appliqué, yet add that extra special touch. Their purpose is to cover seams and add a finished feel to the picture. That doesn't mean they can't be pretty in themselves. They just need to flow with the rest of the project.

Look at the photographs and focus in on the variety of trims used. For ribbons, you'll see satin, satin with a picot edge, grosgrain, taffeta, moire taffeta, and velvet. (When picking out ribbons, keep them in scale with your project. Narrower ribbons—one-sixteenth and one-eighth inch—are used in many of the tiny spots on these projects. Most of the time, the ribbon width won't go above one-half inch.) Laces come flat or gathered. The flat ones are easier to use. Select laces with individual motifs that can be cut up and used as decoration. You'll need some trims that can curve, so check their flexibility before purchasing. Look in bridal departments for lace appliqués. Upholstery stores are full of braids that can add a nice textural effect. Rattail cording (round satin cord) is great for curves. Ribbon roses and buttons can add another dimension to the picture. Many antique stores have old trims from hats and dresses that will add just the right touch to a nostalgic picture. This is a place to use some of those special treasures you have been saving.

Don't forget the hobby store. On the white angel (Photo 6), we used iron-on studs to trim the wing. Beads, miniature bells, tiny cloth flowers, and such can work well with certain themes.

Once you get the feel of trimmings, and once you catch that excitement, you'll be discovering new possibilities everywhere! Think of embellishment as a means to hide imperfections. It masks your seams and creates an illusion of something that doesn't appear glued. In essence, it mirrors the overall design statement without labeling it with a specific technique.

Necessities

As you consider embarking on the projects ahead, be assured that you probably already have everything needed. Most likely you'll find all the "necessities" already in your sewing basket or kitchen drawer, or on your desk. And with two of us working on these projects, we've been able to compile a complete yet streamlined list of essentials. One piece of advice, though: gather these items first, before you actually begin ironing and sewing. There's nothing worse than having to stop in the middle of the fun part to find a clothespin, or to sharpen that pencil.

MATERIALS NEEDED FOR PICTURE CONSTRUCTION

- Sharp scissors
- Paper scissors
- 6" ruler
- Tape measure
- Tacky Glue (such as Aleene's Original™)
- Round toothpicks
- Clothespins (spring-style)
- Sharp pencil
- Chopsticks or unsharpened pencil (for poking in stuffing)
- Paper-backed fusible webbing (such as Wonder-Under™ or Heat 'n Bond™)
- Tear-away stabilizer for appliqué (such as Stitch-N-Tear™)
- Iron and ironing board (or other ironing surface)
- Invisible thread for machine quilting
- Thin needlepunch batting (such as Thermolam™ or Crafty Fleece™)
- 3 oz. bonded quilt batting
- Lightweight pressing cloth
- Teflon™ pressing sheet to protect the ironing board (optional)

MATERIALS NEEDED FOR FRAMING

- Straping tape
- Clothespins (spring-style)
- ⅛" foam core board
- 3 oz. bonded quilt batting
- Small nails
- Small hammer
- Exacto™ knife

Construction

Prepare a comfortable work space at a table or counter with your ironing board close by, or set up your iron on a towel near your work surface. Read through all the instructions before you begin and look closely at the illustrations to help you understand the process. Before I begin working, I cut small pieces (6" to 10") of any yardage I've chosen. It's much easier to work with these smaller pieces of fabric. Press wrinkles out of the fabrics.

1. Enlarge or reduce the design on a copy machine, before you begin, to make it fit your frame or space.
2. Trace the appliqué design onto the paper-backed fusible webbing with the smooth paper side toward you. Use a ruler to mark any straight lines. You might want to put a "T" at the top of each piece for future reference (Figure 1). With your paper scissors, cut around the outer edge of the design only. Do not cut it apart.

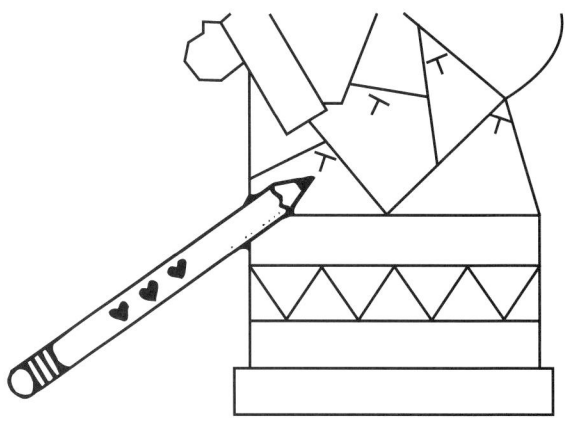

FIG. 1

3. Cut the background fabric according to the specifications list on each individual project. Cutting the pieces a little larger gives you the flexibility of later changing your mind on outer edge trims or on framing.

4. Place the paper pattern, with the rough (webbing) side facing you, on the background fabric. Center the design by measuring from the outside edges of the fabric to the paper edge until you're satisfied with the placement (Figure 2). Remember, the design will automatically reverse itself when you fuse. Look at Photo 7. Compare the finished Santa to the pattern. See how it reverses itself? Any of the symmetrical designs, such as the layered heart, will remain the same. That's why you position the paper with the webbing side up. (Just trust me—I know this is hard to visualize.) With a pencil, make a tiny dot just inside the edge of the paper on the background fabric (Figure 3). These are reference points to aid in proper placement of your design. This is an essential step because even with some of the simplest patterns, it's easy to get off a bit.

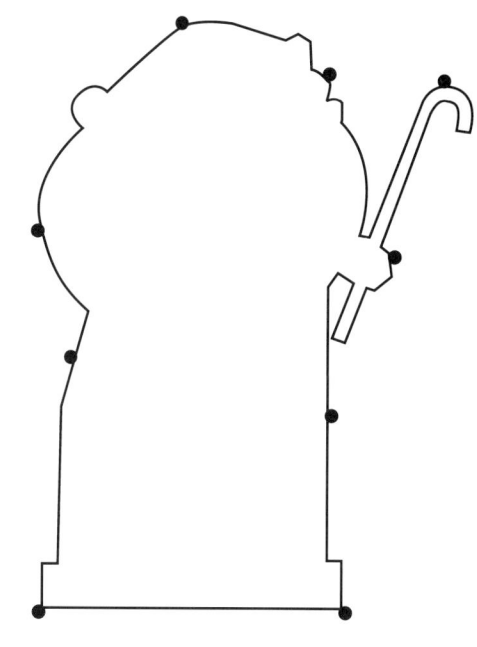

FIG. 3

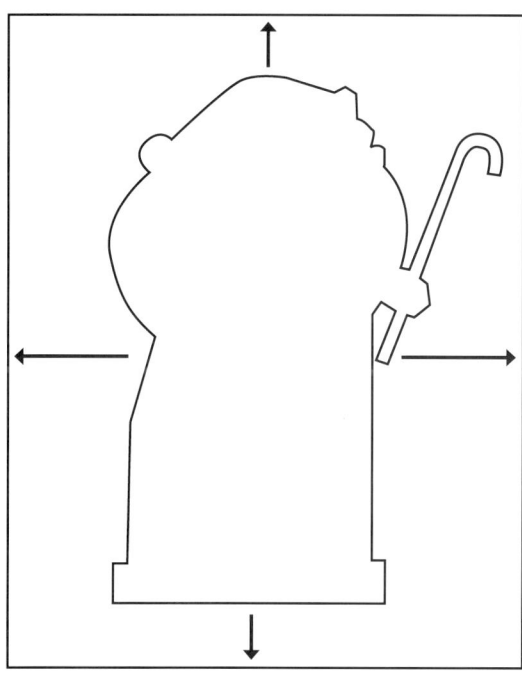

FIG. 2

5. It's generally easier to begin at the bottom of the design. Cut one section only from the paper-backed fusible webbing picture. Place the webbing side down on the wrong side of your chosen fabric (Figure 4). You may want to use a Teflon pressing cloth under your fabric to protect the ironing board. Use the light pressing cloth on top of the webbing. Press according to the instructions on your webbing. With your fabric scissors, cut around the paper edge. Place it in position on the background. Do not remove the paper yet. (This is when you need to remember that the design reverses itself. Turn over the paper pattern with the webbing side facing you, if necessary.)

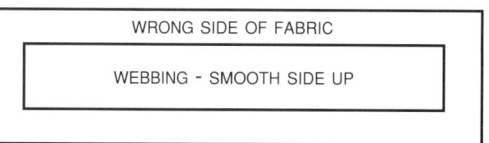

FIG. 4

6. Continue this process until all the pieces are cut and in place. Don't agonize too long over what is next to what. It's the overall effect you're after. If you find you don't like one of your fabrics, cut a new piece of paper-backed webbing and fuse it to a different fabric.
7. Now you're ready to peel the paper off the pieces and position them on the background. The pieces should butt up against each other (Figure 5). There may be gaps created from fabric that is slightly stretched in the peeling-off process. That's okay. Trims will cover the gap. Once everything is in position, place a pressing cloth over the pieces. Press in an up-and-down motion (not a back-and-forth motion). Make sure the pieces are fused down. Re-iron anything that seems loose. Isn't that easy!

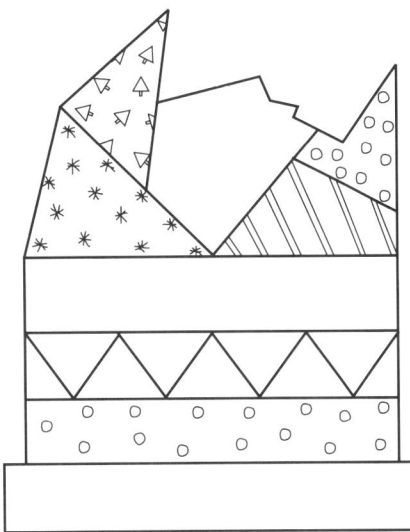

FIG. 5

8. Place your trimmings on the work surface. Get a couple of toothpicks in hand. Squirt a small amount of glue on a piece of scrap paper.
9. Trims are cut piece by piece. Begin placing trims in the smaller areas and work to the larger ones. Then the seams will always cover each other (Figure 6). Cut one piece of trim at a time. Place a small amount of glue on the seamline with the toothpick. Remember that tacky glue dries clear. Place the trim on the glue. Repeat this process until all the trims are in place. On curved areas, it may be necessary to clip flat lace at each design repeat so the lace will lie flat.

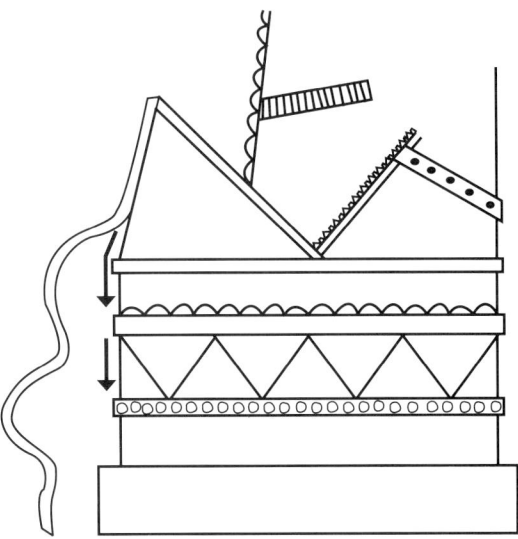

FIG. 6

10. Extra embellishment may now be added—buttons, bows, pearls, or whatever. Or you may wait until the background fabric is stretched around your mounting board. Sometimes when you embellish heavily, adding them after mounting prevents distortion. When gluing buttons and beads in place, dab the glue where you want the button. Let the glue "set up" until it's thick. Then stick the button in place. Think of the glue as a little like mud! The button can be angled or glued on its side if you let the glue set up properly. Remember, the glue dries clear. Pearls and beads can either be sewed on or glued in place as the buttons are.
11. To make bows: Shape the bow between your fingers, add glue with a toothpick where the ribbons overlap, and put a clothespin on the intersection of the loop until it dries (Figure 7).

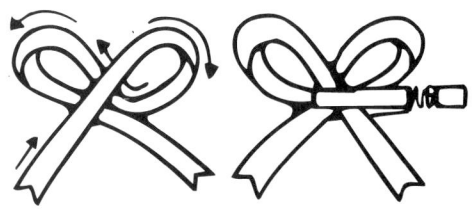

FIG. 7

To make loops: Loop the ribbon in your fingers, add glue with a toothpick where the ribbons overlap, and put a clothespin in the loop until it dries (Figure 8).

FIG. 8

Continuous loops are another idea. The border on the pillow (Photo 2) shows the use of continuous loops with the addition of buttons. You will need three times as much ribbon as the length of the space you are filling. At your sewing machine, fold over a one-inch loop. (I don't measure, I just eyeball it.) Then stitch a few stitches and form another loop. The ribbons butt up to each other (Figure 9). One loop forms to the right and the next to the left. Continue this until you have enough loops to trim the project. To attach the loops to the project, fold them on the stitching line, going in one direction and top-stitch in place. Then the buttons are added.

FIG. 9

To make streamers: Use two or more narrow ribbons. Try playing with the ribbons until they flow right. Sometimes you need to turn or twist them a different way. Place a dot of glue where you want them to attach to the fabric. Use a straight pin on each side of the glue spot to hold the ribbons down until they dry (Figure 10). Roses, buttons, or beads can then be added on that spot.

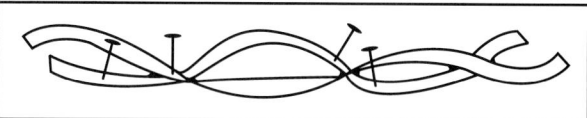

FIG. 10

12. Most pictures need that final trim around the edge to finish them off. Look at the photographs. Sometimes it is a subtle thin ribbon, or a contrasting cord, or a decorative lace. Cords curve well so they will work particularly nicely on a curved edge. Wait until the last minute to cut the raw edge of the cord to prevent excessive fraying. Dab a little extra glue on the raw edges.
13. Some of the pictures have borders. General information on borders is in the section on "Borders and Bindings." Specific details are offered in the individual project instructions.

Machine Appliqué

Machine appliqué is the process where the sewing machine sews close stitches about ⅛" to ¼" apart. It is a very effective way to stitch pictorial images to a background. The stitching around the edge of the design looks like satin stitches.

In all of our machine-appliquéd projects, the designs have been fused in place with paper-backed fusible webbing. This means that they are firmly in place on the background fabric. Place a stabilizer behind the background fabric, under the appliqué, while it is being machine appliquéd. My favorite is a tear-away product that looks like interfacing but isn't. It holds the fabric in place while you stitch close together. A rippling effect that you won't like will result on your appliqué work if you don't use something. Typing paper can also be used, but it has a tendency to weaken the stitches when you tear it away.

Make sure your sewing machine is in good working condition before you begin. I always have the tension adjusted before any big appliqué project.

Test the stitch width before you start. Take into consideration the scale of the project. Change the color of the thread if your appliqué colors change drastically. Take a look at the Bunny and Bear quilts (Photos 17 and 19) to see examples of what we did.

As you approach the inside V of a design, stitch beyond it, as shown in Figure 11; leave the needle on the inside edge, lift the presser foot, and turn the fabric. This makes a clean V shape. As you approach the outside of the V, leave the needle in the fabric on the outside, and turn the fabric. As I round a curve, I move the fabric slowly while the stitching is progressing fast. This way my stitches are even. The more you practice machine appliqué, the more improved your technique will become. We have only used machine appliqué on a few of the projects in this book, but that doesn't mean you can't use it on most of them. You be the creative person.

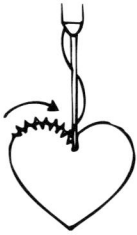

FIG. 11

Dimensional Fusing

For additional dimension in your appliqué, use dimensional fusing on certain pieces and patterns. On the angel dress (Photo 9), for example, cut two pieces of webbing for the shape. Fuse the fabric to Thermolam. Trim away any fuzzy bits that may show. Using the remaining piece of webbing, apply it to the Thermolam side and fuse into place on the appliqué. This process creates a dimensional or raised effect.

Borders and Bindings

Several of our projects have borders; here's a very simple method of applying them. Look at Figure 12, and you'll see that the side borders are added first. The top and bottom borders come last. Press the seams toward the outside of the project.

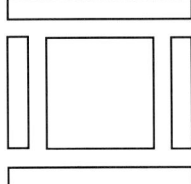

FIG. 12

In the instance of the Heavenly Angel (Photo 6), the gold lamé border also acts as the binding for the wall quilt. The binding on the bordered fan quilt (Photo 16) is the same as the background fabric so it is hardly noticeable.

On most bindings shown in these projects, the fabric is pulled around to the wrong side of the quilt, turned under ¼", then handstitched in place. You could easily machine stitch it if you like. This process leaves a ¼" binding showing on the right side of the quilt. It's quick and easy!

Quilting

Both machine quilting and hand quilting have been incorporated into our projects. First, mark the quilt if the designs are other than outline stitching. Test the marking pencil or tool for removability before you begin. Marks from a very fine lead pencil will almost disappear by the time you finish. That is what was used on the bordered fan quilt. I can't recommend any one marking product since each product will react differently to your particular fabric and the finish on it. Just test it first.

Quilting is the process in which the batting is sandwiched between the quilt top and the backing. The layers are then pinned or basted together. Hand or machine stitches bind these layers. The quilting process creates a raised or sculptured look on the surface.

To machine quilt, begin by using invisible thread in the top and matching thread in the bobbin. Set the stitch length at 10 to 12 stitches per inch. You may want to put your walking foot on the sewing machine if you have one. It will help the three layers feed evenly through the machine. Take your time as you work through the stitching. Working on a table that is large enough to hold the whole project really helps. When you're finished, pull thread ends to the back of the quilt, and tie them off.

Hand quilting uses small hand stitches to hold the three layers together. The quilt can be put in a frame if necessary, but I've found these smaller quilts are easier to quilt when they're not in a frame. Be sure the layers are basted together, using stitches about three inches apart. To begin hand quilting, knot a single thread and pull it through the top layer of fabric so that the knot disappears. You may need to scratch the knot to help it start working through. The needle should travel as straight as it can through the three layers and come back up straight. The thickness of the batting and the size of the needle will determine how far apart the stitches are. I like the thinner battings for hand quilting and I use at least a size 10 needle. The first few stitches are always awkward. It takes about fifteen minutes to get into a rhythm.

The hand quilting on all of our projects is more decorative than utilitarian since most of these projects are wallhangings. Hand quilting enhances the design, though, and adds a little more love.

Pillows

Finishing pillows is a fairly straightforward process. A pillow back must be cut the same size as the front. If a ruffle or cording is included it should be sewn to the front of the pillow at this time. See Figure 13 for placement.

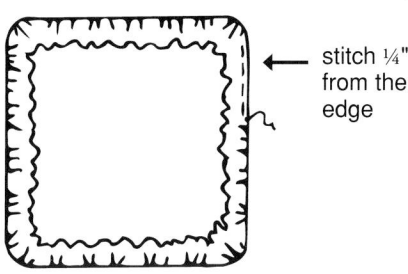

← stitch ¼" from the edge

FIG. 13

Place the right sides of the pillow front and back together. Stitch around the edges, leaving at least a 4" opening on one side for turning it right side out. If a ruffle or cording has been stitched on the front, then stitch on top of that line. Trim off excess fabric around the edges and clip the corners. Turn the pillow to the right side.

To stuff the pillow, pull apart a small amount of stuffing at a time and push it into the far corners of the pillow. A chopstick or unsharpened pencil can be helpful in the stuffing process. You'll be surprised how much stuffing it actually takes. When you're finished stuffing, hand stitch the opening closed.

Framing and Finishing

You will see a great variety of framing in the photos of these projects, from professionally done frames to quilts hung on rods. Our examples are wall pieces, for the most part, so the room setting will dictate what will work best. Here are some general instructions for the do-it-yourself framer.

Be on the lookout for frames wherever you are: antique shops, the variety store, frame shops, garage sales, wherever. Many times the frame itself will determine the style of picture you do. The Victorian Santa (Photo 13) just demanded an old-fashioned, antique-looking frame. On the other hand, a plain white frame for Pastel House and Heart (Photo 12) was the perfect choice to set off the soft pastels of that more delicate-feeling project.

You may need to adjust the size of the picture to fill the frame you have. All the patterns can be reduced or enlarged on a copy machine.

1. If you have purchased a new frame, there will already be a piece of backing cardboard that you can use to mount the picture on. Otherwise, buy some thin, foam core board at an art supply store. It's easy to cut with an Exacto knife or an Olfa™ rotary cutter. I use my ruler that I use for cutting strips for quilting projects. It works great. Any kind of cardboard will work as long as it doesn't bend easily, but I prefer the foam core. When you cut the cardboard or core board, make it ⅛" less than the frame opening on all sides. Cut thin batting the exact size of the cardboard.
2. Center the picture on the cardboard. Measure the sides, top, and bottom, and place a straight pin in the middle of each side, and in the top and bottom at the edge of the cardboard (Figure 14). This marks where the cardboard will come on the edge of the picture. Trim off excess fabric one inch from the pins.

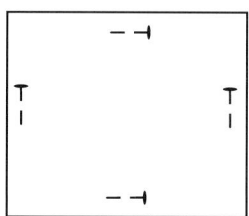

FIG. 14

3. Put the picture right side down on the table. Place the quilt batting on the fabric, centering it inside the pins, then place the cardboard on top of the batting. Squirt about a one-inch line of glue in the middle of each side. Put one of your hands firmly on the middle of the cardboard and press down (Figure 15). With the other hand, gently pull the fabric over the edge of the cardboard into the glue. A clothespin can be used to hold the fabric in place while it's drying. Now pull the fabric firmly around the edge of the opposite side and secure it with a clothespin. The straight pins you placed earlier on the edges will help you in positioning the fabric. Continue this process on the top and bottom.

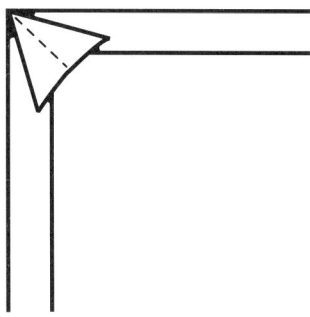

FIG. 16

5. Place the picture in the frame and secure it with tiny nails, as necessary.

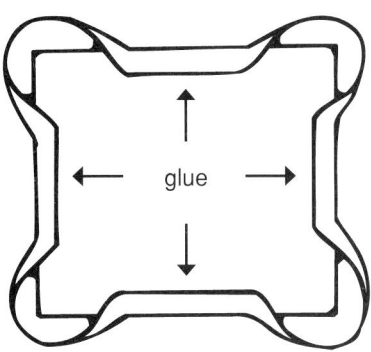

FIG. 15

4. Now you are ready to work toward the corners. Squirt some glue from where you left off, to the corners. Work the fabric over the edge of the cardboard and at the same time pull it toward the corners to avoid any buckling of the fabric. Look at Figure 16 to see how to fold the fabric at the corners. Clothespins work great for holding the fabric in place while the glue dries.

1. The Friendship Fan

As friendships grow more precious with time, so do old lace and buttons. With lives so busy and complicated, it's comforting to look at the past—the simplicity of Grandma's buttons and lace—and to think of old friendships that will last forever. A rounded lace collar makes up the center curved section of this fan. The assortment of buttons works with ribbon snips to bring together a charming nostalgic statement. This is a visible remembrance from the past to give to other family members and dear friends. The ornate frame was the starting point for the choice of fabrics and accessories in this picture.

Design runs the same size as the pattern shown. (Refer to pattern on page 52 and photo on page 21.)

Materials

½ yd. of background fabric
⅛ yd. each of five fabrics for fan sections
⅛ yd. of large floral contrasting fabric
10" long x 2" wide lace collar or other lace that will curve enough for the space
½ yd. of ½" flat lace for edge of fans
⅔ yd. of ⅛" ribbon for outside edges of upper fans
⅔ yd. of ⅛" ribbon for interior of upper fans
⅓ yd. of ⅛" ribbon for lower fan wedges
6" of ¹⁄₁₆" ribbon for bottom fan
approximately 55 buttons for embellishment
⅓ yd. of paper-backed fusible webbing
½ yd. of 3 oz. quilt batting

Instructions

1. Cut the background fabric to a piece that measures 13" x 16".
2. Read the general instructions on appliqué, in the chapter on "The Basics," before you begin. Using the pattern, cut the fabric pieces you need; then fuse them in place.
3. Read the general instructions on application of trims (also in "The Basics"), then begin adding the embellishments you've settled on. Note that depending on the collar pieces you've chosen, the upper edge of the collar piece will likely overlap the fan borders above.
4. This picture was framed following the instructions in the section on "Framing and Finishing."

Finished size: 11" x 14".

2. Quilter's Garden

We titled this design Quilter's Garden because it has a pieced gardeny feel to it. It's planted with bits of ribbon, buttons, and bows. What a terrific way to share from your garden of scraps! And it's a wonderfully fitting gift for a quilting friend.

Design runs larger than the pattern shown. *Set the copy machine at 130%.* (Refer to pattern on page 53 and photo on page 22.)

MATERIALS

- ½ yd. each of background fabric and backing for the pillow
- scraps of eight to ten fabrics for piecing
- 1½ yds. of ½" ribbon for the edge of the patchwork on pillow
- ½ yd. of ⅜" ribbon for the bow
- 3¼ yds. (approximately) total of scraps of narrow ribbons (¼" and ⅛"), laces, and cording for the patchwork
- pearls, buttons, and ribbon roses (optional)
- 5 yds. of ¼" double-faced satin ribbon for the ruffle
- 80 to 100 old or new buttons of various sizes and shapes to stitch around the edge
- 12 oz. of fiber fill for stuffing the pillow
- ½ yd. of paper-backed fusible webbing
- ½ yd. of 3 oz. bonded quilt batting

INSTRUCTIONS

1. Cut two pieces of quilt batting and two pieces of background fabric, each 14½" x 16". Use one of the background fabrics for the appliqué design, the other for the pillow back.
2. Read the general instructions for appliqué and trimming (in "The Basics") before beginning.
3. Layer the appliqué design on one of the pieces of background fabric. Machine quilt around the edge of the design ¼" from the edge of the ribbon border. Stitch a second line the width of the presser foot away from the first line of stitching.
4. To make the loops for the ruffle, follow the instructions in the section on "Trimming."
5. To finish the pillow, follow the general instructions in the section on "Pillows."
6. Stitch buttons around the edge of the pillow where the ribbon and fabric intersect. Be sure to knot after each button.

Finished size: 13½" x 15".

3. Evening Quilter's Garden

Our evening quilter's garden has a nighttime glow about it. For the friend who has antiques, this is a perfect gift.

Design runs larger than the pattern shown. *Set the copy machine at 112%.* (Refer to pattern on page 53 and photo on page 23.)

MATERIALS

Except for the size being a little smaller, this Evening Quilter's Garden requires much the same amounts of fabrics and trimmings as does the previous project, Quilter's Garden.
- ½ yd. of Thermolam
- 1⅝ yds. of 1" ribbon for frame
- 1½ yds. of ⅛" ribbon for frame
- 12" x 13" foam core board for mounting

INSTRUCTIONS

1. Cut the background fabric to a piece that measures 15" x 16".
2. Follow the instructions for Quilter's Garden for appliqué and trimming.
3. Cut the Thermolam to a piece that measures 12" x 13". Center it behind the picture.
4. Glue the ribbon for the frame to the top and bottom. Its outside edge should come to the edge of the Thermolam underneath. Glue ribbon to the sides. Let the ends of the ribbon overlay about an inch.
5. Following the instructions in the section on "Framing and Finishing," mount the picture on the foam core board. This style of picture looks particularly good if it protrudes from the wall when hung. To achieve this, glue little squares of Thermolam on the corners of the back of the frame. It may take two or three layers.

Finished size: 12" x 13".

(Instructions continued on page 25.)

1. The Friendship Fan

2. Quilter's Garden

3. Evening Quilter's Garden
4. Oriental Fan
5. Crazy Patch Heart

6. Heavenly Angel

7. Old-fashioned Santa

4. Oriental Fan

Soft peaches and creams were chosen to give the fans an Oriental flavor. The embellishment is focused on the curving center panel with ribbons winding in and out of the antique pearl buttons. Opalescent beads dot each fan, carrying out the simplicity of the design. The old pearl buttons have been dyed with peach Rit dye to change them to a subtle peach color. Flat lace decorates the outer edges of the fan. This picture is a present to myself. We all need those sometimes.

Design runs the same size as the pattern shown. (Refer to pattern on page 52 and photo on page 23.)

MATERIALS

- ½ yd. of background fabric
- ⅛ yd. each of five solids for fans
- ⅛ yd. of fabric for upper section of fan
- ⅛ yd. of fabric for the middle section
- 5" x 7" scrap of fabric for the lower section
- 1 yd. of narrow cording for middle section
- 1 yd. of ⅜" flat lace for small fans
- 1½ yds. of ⅜" satin ribbon with a picot edge for lower fan and middle section
- 2 yds. of ⅛" satin ribbon for small fans and middle section
- ½ yd. of ⅛" satin ribbon for outer edges of large fan
- 1½ yds. of ¹⁄₁₆" satin ribbon for small fan wedges
- approximately 20 buttons (½" in size or smaller)
- 6 beads, about ¼"
- ⅓ yd. of paper-backed fusible webbing

INSTRUCTIONS

1. Cut the background fabric to a piece that measures 15" x 17".
2. Read the general instructions in "The Basics" on appliqué and application of trims before you begin.
3. This fan was professionally framed but easily could be framed by you.

Finished size before framing: 13" x 15".
Finished size, including the mat, after framing: 19" x 21".

5. Crazy Patch Heart

Black and grape is the best way to describe the colors in this crazy patch heart. If you look closely at the variety of fabric, you will see large and small prints, some with so much white in them that they appear gray. This picture lends itself for birthdays, Mother's Day, or just "You are a Special Person in My Life Day." By using traditional reds and greens and topping with a large bow, you'll find the heart takes on an ornament-like look for a great holiday giveable.

Design runs the same size as the pattern shown. (Refer to pattern on page 54 and photo on page 23.)

MATERIALS

- ½ yd. of background fabric
- 6" x 8" scrap of black for heart
- scraps of black and grape prints (I used 7 blacks and 7 grapes)
- 1¾ yds. of narrow upholstery trim
- ⅓ yd. of paper-backed fusible webbing

INSTRUCTIONS

1. Cut the background fabric to a piece that measures 15" x 16".
2. Before beginning, read the general instructions for appliqué and trimming in the chapter on "The Basics." This design is a mirror image of itself although you would never know it. The pattern shows half of the design. You will need to turn over the paper and trace the other half.
3. This picture was professionally framed, but easily could be framed by you.

Finished size: 13" x 14".

6. Heavenly Angel

When I first saw this drawing, I visualized it in whites, silvers, and golds, all to celebrate the joy of the holiday season. An embossed white cotton was used for the background fabric. The fabrics in the angel range from moire taffeta to satin to eyelet and polished cottons. Look for a variety of textures. The angel's hair is made up of tiny ribbon roses glued in place (just cut off the green leaves). A mixture of flat lace trim and ribbons adorns her dress. The border at the bottom of the wallhanging repeats the crazy patch motif. Clouds are machine quilted subtly into the background to give a heavenly effect. Gold lamé narrowly borders the angel wallhanging. Because Christmas colors have expanded beyond the traditional red and green, this angel is a rich and refreshing addition to anyone's holiday decor.

Design runs larger than the pattern shown. *Set copy machine at 120%.* (Refer to pattern on pages 56-59 and photo on page 24.)

Materials

⅝ yd. of background fabric
fabrics for angel:
 ¼ yd. each of two fabrics for wing and border
 ¼ yd. each of two fabrics for angel dress and border
 scraps of four other fabrics for angel and border
 ¼ yd. of gold lamé for horn and binding
 scrap of light peach for face and hand
⅝ yd. of backing fabric
1 yd. of ⅝" ribbon for top of border and trimming
1¾ yds. of ⅛" ribbon to outline the angel
1½ yds. total of three or four other narrow
 decorative ribbons to trim angel and dowel
1½ yds. of ½" ribbon to trim
½ yd. of tiny pearls on a string
½ yd. of large pearls (can be purchased in a package)
16 small ribbon roses for hair
1 yd. of ¼" flat heart lace trim for angel and border
3" of ¼" flat lace trim for collar
7 motifs from lace to cut apart and trim the halo and border
18 iron-on silver studs
22" dowel, ½" in diameter
gold or silver spray paint for dowel
extra trims for dowels (optional)
½ yd. paper-backed fusible webbing
⅝ yd. of 3 oz. bonded quilt batting

Instructions

1. Cut the background fabric, backing and batting, each piece measuring 19¼" x 20¾". Position the 3" x 20¾" border at the bottom edge. Mark where the border is to go. Center the angel in the space remaining. Read the general instructions for appliqué and trimming before beginning (in the section on "The Basics").
2. After the angel and border are fused in place, trace the clouds onto the background with a fine pencil.
3. Layer the quilt. Machine or hand quilt the clouds and around the edge of the angel (see Photo 6).
4. Cut the lamé binding: two sides, each 1½" x 19¼"; top and bottom, each 1½" x 22¾". Add the binding to the sides, top, and bottom using a ¼" seam allowance. Before hand stitching the binding to the back of the quilt, add the loops for the dowel.
5. Using a ½" ribbon or the gold lamé, cut four strips ½" x 4" for dowel holders. Place these an equal distance apart along the top of the wallhanging (Figure 17). The ribbon is folded in half and the raw edges butt up to the top edge, as shown. Pin in place. Machine stitch across the ribbons.

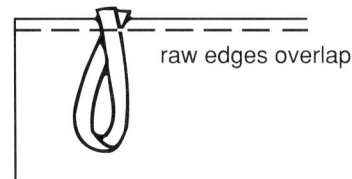

FIG. 17

6. Hand stitch the binding in place.
7. Lightly press around the edges. If too much heat is used, the batting will melt. Tack the ribbon loops to the lamé border.
8. Glue ribbons and trims to the dowel. Look at Photo 6 for ideas.
9. The eye is a small snipped corner of black ribbon. The cheek shading is achieved by lightly coloring with an oil-based colored pencil, or you can use make-up blush.

Finished size: 19¼" x 20¾".

7. Old-fashioned Santa

Old-fashioned Santa creeps silently along, bringing with him the gift of sweet memories past. Framed in a simple shadow box, he appears very dimensional. The mini-tree and ornaments finish off the picture box effect. Remember, a Christmas picture is always welcomed and can be given year-round.

Design runs larger than the pattern shown. *Set the copy machine at 145%.* (Refer to pattern on pages 60-61 and photo on page 24.)

MATERIALS

⅔ yd. of background fabric
⅛ yd. of fabric for sleeve and robe
¼ yd. of fabric for bag and glove
⅛ yd. of fabric for hat
⅛ yd. of fabric for trimming hat, sleeve, and robe
7 scraps for remaining patchwork
1½" x 2" scrap of fabric for the face
2½" x 9" scrap of fabric for the staff
1 yd. of ¼" ribbon to outline body
10" of ½" ribbon for bottom band
¼ yd. of metallic cording for staff bow
7 pieces of narrow lace and ribbon each measuring 9" for trim on bottom bands
scraps of narrow lace, ribbon, beads, and small buttons to trim interior of Santa robe, sleeve, and hat
roving for beard
½ yd. of paper-backed fusible webbing
invisible thread
⅔ yd. of Thermolam
miniature tree and Christmas ornaments for shadow box (optional)

INSTRUCTIONS

1. Cut the background fabric and Thermolam each to a piece that measures 18" x 22½". Follow the general instructions for appliqué and trimming given in "The Basics."
2. Layer Santa on the Thermolam and pin in place. Machine zigzag with narrow stitches around the edge of Santa with invisible thread.
3. Frame according to the instructions in the section on "Framing and Finishing."

Finished size: 16" x 20½".

8. Christmas Tree

What a wonderful gift...a decorated tree below a glowing star! (Not to mention the row of tiny packages beribboned below.) The construction leaves ample time left over for your other Christmas commitments, yet glows with the special warmth that only a quilt can produce. Our old-fashioned Santa appears as a greeting tag on the plate of cookies.

Design runs larger than the pattern shown. *Set the copy machine at 120%.* (Refer to pattern on pages 62-63 and photo on page 33.)

MATERIALS

⅝ yd. of fabric for background and backing
8 to 10 scraps of fabric at least 4" x 5" for tree and packages
4" x 4" gold lamé for star
1 yd. each of five ribbons, ¼" to ⅜", for ties and package bows
scraps of flat trims and lace for tree
1 yd. of thin gold metallic cording for tree bows
⅛ yd. of ornamental braid to cut up for tree
1 yd. of 1/16" ribbon for outer edge of tree
¼ yd. of 1/16" ribbon for tree trunk
12 to 15 miscellaneous buttons for tree
½ yd. of 3 oz. bonded quilt batting
½ yd. of paper-backed fusible webbing
gold quilting thread
13½" dowel
gold metallic spray paint

INSTRUCTIONS

1. Cut the background fabric, backing, and batting, each piece measuring 13" x 20½". Read the general instructions on fusing and trimming in "The Basics."
2. Cut six 2" squares of webbing, and fuse them to the back of the package fabric. Fuse the row of packages ½" up from the bottom of the fabric and ½" in from each side.
3. Center the tree and star pieces above the gifts, leaving ¾" between the packages and the tree trunk. Proceed with appliqué and trimming according to the instructions in "The Basics."
4. Transfer and extend the quilting lines coming from the star. Refer to the pattern pieces.
5. Trim the tree and glue the bows on the packages. The bows on the tree are just metallic cord looped around several times and tied in the center, then glued in place.

6. Cut five sets of ribbons, each 10" long, for the ties for the dowel. We used a variety of ribbons to repeat the theme of the bows on the packages at the bottom of the wallhanging. Pin the ribbon sets at even intervals along the top (Figure 18). The ribbons will be enclosed in a seam.

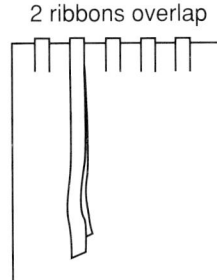

FIG. 18

7. Place the right side of the picture on the right side of the backing. Place these two fabrics on the quilt batting. Stitch around the edges of the quilt ½" from the edge, leaving an opening 4" wide at the side for turning. Trim the seam allowances to ¼", and clip the corners.
8. Turn to the right side. Lightly press the edges. (Be careful—too much heat will melt the batting.) Close the opening by hand stitching it shut.
9. Machine quilt with gold metallic thread.
10. Spray paint the dowel, then (when it's dry) tie the ribbons to the dowel.

Finished size: 12" x 19½".

9. Celestial Angel

This angel sings of a celestial message. Her song is a year-round reminder of brotherly love not just to be heard at Christmas. The dimensional fusing technique adds interest to the angel's gown and halo area.

Design runs the same size as the pattern shown. (Refer to pattern on pages 56-59 and photo on page 33.)

MATERIALS

Fabric requirements are the same as for the earlier project, the Heavenly Angel, though this project is a little smaller.
⅓ yd. of ½" gold metallic ribbon for dress
⅔ yd. of ½" flat gold metallic trim for halo and dress
1 yd. of ⅛" gold curveable metallic ribbon for streamer, halo, and wing
⅓ yd. of narrow silver cord for horn
1 yd. of ⅛" black ribbon for angel
⅓ yd. of ⅛" black braid for wing
scrap of ¼" gold trim for sleeve
11 gold star studs, each ¼" in size
25 beads
gray roving for hair
½ yd. of paper-backed fusible webbing
⅝ yd. of 3 oz. bonded quilt batting

INSTRUCTIONS

1. Cut the background fabric to a piece that measures 18" x 22".
2. Fuse the angel sections following the general instructions in "The Basics."
3. To add dimension to parts of the angel (robe section, hearts on halo, and border of halo), use the dimensional fusing technique described in "The Basics." For further dimension, a small square of Thermolam is glued under the dimensionally fused pieces to raise them off the base fabric.
4. Add trims (see Photo 9) following the general trimming instructions from "The Basics." The eye is a small snipped corner of black ribbon. The cheek shading is achieved by lightly coloring with an oil-based pencil, or you can use make-up blush.
5. Frame according to framing and finishing instructions in "The Basics."

Finished size: 16" x 20".

10. Corner Fan

What better gift for the home than a striking fabric picture such as this. The construction is simple, just done on a large scale. Individual floral motifs extracted from the border create central points of interest. The grid effect on the fan is achieved by utilizing squares in a large checked fabric. It all makes for a very warm yet contemporary look.

Design runs larger than the pattern shown. *Set the copy machine at 120%.* (Refer to pattern on page 55 and photo on page 34.)

MATERIALS

(Refer to Figure 19 for yardage placement.)
1⅛ yds. of fabric for Pieces A and I
¼ yd. of fabric for Piece B
⅔ yd. of fabric for Piece C
⅛ yd. each of fabric for Pieces D, E, F, and G
⅛ yd. of fabric for Pieces H and J
5 yds. of ⅛" ribbon (++++ in Figure 20)
4½ yds. of ¼" ribbon (xxxxx in Figure 20)
8¼ yds. of ⅛" ribbon (••••• in Figure 20)
2½ yds. of ⅛" flat lace (oooo in Figure 20)
2¼ yds. of paper-backed fusible webbing

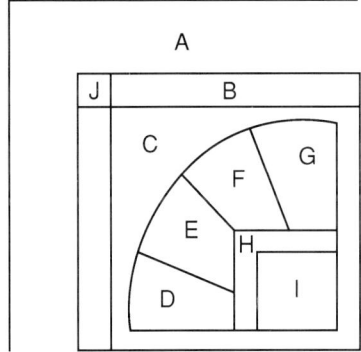

FIG. 19

INSTRUCTIONS

1. Cut the background fabric (Piece A) to a piece that measures 28" x 38". Then prepare these pieces:
    Cut 17 of Piece B, each 1" x 9"
    Cut 6 of Piece C, each 9" x 9"
    Cut 6 each of Pieces D, E, F, and G
    Cut 6 of Piece H, each 4" x 4"
    Cut 6 of Piece I, each 3" x 3"
    Cut 12 of Piece J, each 1" x 1"

2. The fused appliqué on this quilt is done in layers. The fans are fused first. Begin with Piece C on the bottom, then add D, E, F, G, and H. On top of Piece H put Piece I. Read the general instructions on fusing and trimming in "The Basics."

3. Place the fans on the background fabric (Piece A), coming in 4½" from the edge. Leave 1" between the fans for Pieces J and B. Fuse J and B in place.

4. Glue the trims according to the general instructions in "The Basics."

5. This picture is professionally framed, but it could easily be framed by you following the instructions in the section on "Framing and Finishing."

Finished size: 26" x 36".

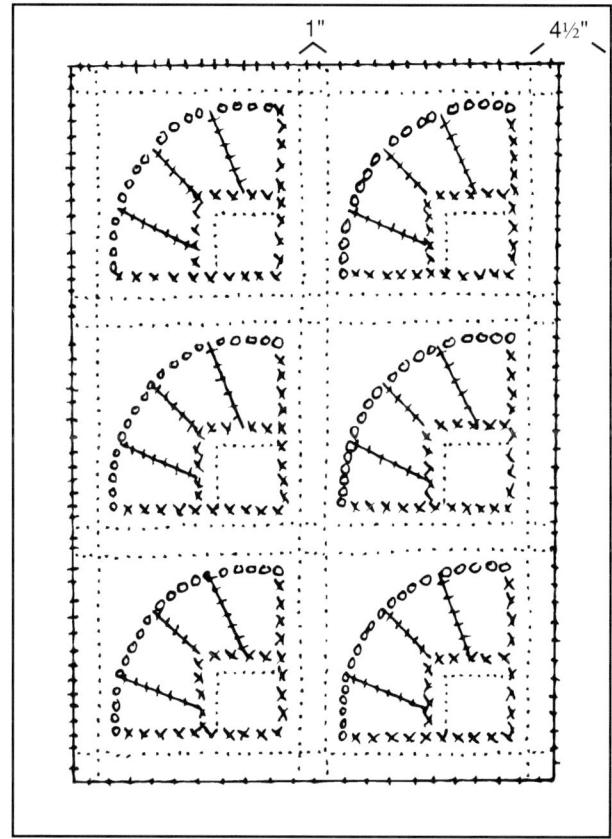

++++ = ⅛" ribbon
xxxxx = ¼" ribbon
••••• = ⅛" ribbon
oooo = ⅛" flat lace

FIG. 20

11. Tulip Fan

This fan is softly reminiscent of Grandmother's day. It combines florals, laces, and ribbon for a definite old-fashioned flair. Grandma would marvel at how a new-fangled technique combined with traditional quilting can bring such lovely results.

Design runs the same size as the pattern shown. (Refer to pattern on page 66 and photo on page 35.)

MATERIALS
⅜ yd. of background fabric
4 pieces of fabric, each 4" x 5", for the fan
3 small scraps of fabric for flower and leaf
⅝ yd. of ⅛" ribbon for fan divisions
¼ yd. of ¹⁄₁₆" ribbon for around flower
¼ yd. of ⅛" ribbon for around leaf
½ yd. of ⅜" picot-edged ribbon for bow
20 small beads
3 or 4 small buttons
7 small ribbon roses
6 heart doilies, each 2" x 2", or ½ yd. of 2" lace
⅓ yd. of 3 oz. bonded quilt batting
¼ yd. of paper-backed fusible webbing
hand-quilting thread

INSTRUCTIONS
1. Cut the background fabric to a piece that measures 13" x 16". Proceed in fusing and trimming according to instructions in "The Basics."
2. With a layer of quilt batting behind the appliqué pinned in place, hand quilt according to the design in Figure 21. (There is no backing fabric, only batting and appliqué. This will work fine since it is being framed.)
3. Our picture is professionally framed, but you could easily frame this yourself.

FIG. 21

Finished size: 11" x 14".

12. Pastel House and Heart

The blue lacy fabric was the inspiration for the choice of colors in this picture. The raspberry-type pinks were added to highlight the clean look of the blue. This picture is a birthday gift for a dear friend that has a beautiful wedding ring quilt done in these colors in her guest bedroom. Many times a special person will be responsible for the color choices that you make. This has an early spring look to me. It has been professionally framed with a fabric-covered mat. This is one of the simplest designs in the book.

Design runs the same size as the pattern shown. (Refer to pattern on pages 64-65 and photo on page 35.)

MATERIALS
½ yd. of background fabric
½ yd. of fabric for matting and block
5½" x 5½" of fabric for the house
3" x 8" of fabric for the roof and heart
⅛ yd. of fabric for borders
⅛ yd. of fabric for center block and door and window
scraps of fabric for corner grid and chimney
1 yd. of ⅛" ribbon for outside border
1 yd. of ⅛" ribbon for inside border
⅓ yd. of ⅛" ribbon for door and window
½ yd. of ¹⁄₁₆" ribbon for corner grid
½ yd. of ⅜" flat lace for window and center block
1 ribbon rose
½ yd. of paper-backed fusible webbing

INSTRUCTIONS
1. Cut the background fabric to a piece that measures 13" x 18". Position the block 2½" up from the bottom edge.
2. Follow the general instructions for appliqué and application of trims from the chapter on "The Basics."
3. Look at Photo 12 for additional ideas.
4. See, we told you it was simple!

Finished size before framing: 11" x 16".
Finished size with mat and frame: 14½" x 21".

13. Victorian Santa

Santa has a new look in the rose-hued Victorian fabrics. Various shades and textures of rose-colored fabric make up Santa's robe in this Victorian Santa. Gold metallic ribbons and braids laced with pink contribute to the look. Upholstery strip fabric was chosen for the background.

Design runs larger than the pattern shown. *Set the copy machine at 145%.* (Refer to pattern on pages 60-61 and photo on page 36.)

MATERIALS

The fabric requirements are the same as for the Old-fashioned Santa project (Project #7). This Santa does not use the lace trim that Old-fashioned Santa does. Metallic trims were chosen instead. Look closely at Photo 13 for trimming ideas.

INSTRUCTIONS

1. Cut the background fabric to a piece that measures 18" x 22½". Follow the general instructions for fusing and trimmings in "The Basics."
2. This Santa was professionally framed. If you decide to frame him yourself, follow the instructions in the section on "Framing and Finishing."

Finished size: 16" x 20½".

14. Country House and Heart

Our wallhanging welcomes you with a country flair. Its simplicity of style and construction brings together a heartwarming "house warming" gift.

Design runs the same size as the pattern shown. (Refer to pattern on pages 64-65 and photo on page 36.)

MATERIALS

The same amount of yardage is needed for the background, appliqué, and webbing as were needed for the earlier project, Pastel House and Heart (Project #12). No trims are used on this picture, though.

½ yd. of fabric for background and backing
⅛ yd. of fabric for outside border and block border
5½" x 5½" of fabric for the house
3" x 12" of fabric for the roof and corner grid
4" x 5" of fabric for center block and window
4" x 12" of fabric for center heart and corner grid
6" x 7" of fabric for door and block
⅝ yd. of Thermolam
½ yd. of paper-backed fusible webbing
¼ yd. of ⅜" ribbon for loops
invisible thread

INSTRUCTIONS

1. Cut background fabric, backing, and Thermolam each to a piece that measures 12½" x 19".
2. Cut the following outside border fabrics:
    2 strips, each 1½" x 15"
    2 strips, each 1½" x 8½"
    4 corner blocks, each 1½" x 1½"
3. Begin fusing by placing the outside borders ½" from the outside edge of the background fabric (including the corner squares). Fuse these in place. Position the house design ½" from the inside of the border. Continue the fusing process until the entire design is fused. (Check "The Basics" for details.)
4. Place a layer of Thermolam behind the background fabric, and pin it in place. Cut two ribbons, each 4½". Position them at the border. Place the backing on top. Stitch around the two sides and top, enclosing the ribbons in the seams. Clip the corners. Turn to the right side. Hand stitch the opening shut.

Finished size: 11½" x 18".

15. Layered Hearts

15A. Wedding Heart

A silver layered heart softened with ribbon roses and lace is a fitting gift for a wedding or anniversary. The central heart fabric choice is reminiscent of the fresh rose petals in the picture. A touch of machine quilting on cotton fabric is a delightful contrast to the graphic grid background fabric. The best combination of fabrics are sometimes those that are of completely different textures. Opposites do attract!

Design runs the same size as the pattern shown. (Refer to pattern on page 67 and photo on page 37.)

Materials

½ yd. of background fabric
8" x 9" of fabric for large heart
3" x 5" of fabric for lower part of middle heart
4" x 4" of fabric for small heart
¼ yd. of 1½" ribbon for center band
½ yd. of ⅜" ribbon for bow and streamers
½ yd. of ½" ribbon for loops
½ yd. of ¼" trim for lower edge of large heart and loop on bow
⅓ yd. of ¼" ribbon for streamers
⅓ yd. of flat narrow lace for top middle heart
¼ yd. of flat lace for inside lower edge of large heart
⅞ yd. of ½" flat lace for outer edge of large heart
½ yd. of cording for upper edge of large heart
30 small pearls
3 ribbon roses
9 small buttons
⅓ yd. of paper-backed fusible webbing
½ yd. of Thermolam
contrasting thread for machine quilting in the upper heart section
invisible thread

Instructions

1. Cut one piece of background fabric and and one of Thermolam, each measuring 15" x 16". Read the general instructions for fusing and trimming in the chapter on "The Basics."
2. Cut a large heart from both the fabric and webbing. Fuse to the center of the background fabric.
3. Cut the fabric and webbing for the bottom of the middle heart. Fuse in place.
4. Cut webbing 1½" x 8" to fit behind the ribbon for the center band. Fuse the band in place. Cut the small heart, and fuse it over the middle heart.
5. Lay the background fabric over the Thermolam, and pin it in place. Machine quilt in a narrow zigzag stitch with invisible thread on the small heart and the lower middle heart. Lightly pencil in the quilting lines for the upper portion of the heart. Machine quilt with a contrasting color of thread.
6. Glue trims in place.
7. This picture was professionally framed. (And, as always, you can frame these projects yourself— read the section on "Framing and Finishing" first, though.)

Finished size: 13" x 14".

15B. Valentine Heart

Picture this Valentine Heart as a sweet surprise. The ruffled ribbon combined with a sampling of textures of white on white create an almost "iced cake" look. Dimension was obtained by fusing the fabric to the Thermolam, then layering the heart and machine quilting with invisible thread. The coordinating gift tag is found in the chapter on "Wrapping It Up."

Design runs the same size as the pattern shown. (Refer to pattern on page 67 and photo on page 37.)

Materials

½ yd. of background fabric
8" x 9" of fabric for large heart
2" x 6" of fabric for upper part of middle heart
3" x 5" of fabric for lower part of middle heart
4" x 4" of fabric for small heart
¼ yd. of 1" ribbon for center band
¼ yd. of ½" ribbon for center band
¾ yd. of ⅜" ribbon for bow
½ yd. of ½" ribbon for bow
1" round piece of lace for center of bow
⅓ yd. of ¼" flat lace for small heart
¼ yd. of ¼" flat lace for lower part of middle heart
⅞ yd. of 1" pre-ruffled ribbon for outer edge of large heart
⅞ yd. of cording for outer edge of large heart

(Materials list and instructions continued on page 41.)

8. Christmas Tree

9. Celestial Angel

10. Corner Fan

11. Tulip Fan

12. Pastel House and Heart

13. Victorian Santa

14. Country House and Heart

Layered Hearts

15A. Wedding Heart

15B. Valentine Heart

Picture This 37

16. Bordered Fan

17. Bunny Kisses Quilt
18. Bunny Kisses Pillow

Picture This 39

19. Bears and Bow Ties Quilt
20. Bears and Bow Tie Nap Pillow

3 pearl buttons, each ⅜"
1 heart button, ½"
⅓ yd. of paper-backed fusible webbing
½ yd. of Thermolam
invisible thread

INSTRUCTIONS

1. Cut background fabric to a piece that measures 13" x 16". Cut two layers of Thermolam the same size as the background fabric.
2. This design is assembled differently than the other designs. The pieces are layered on each other instead of fitting together like a puzzle. Read the general instructions for fusing and trimming in the chapter on "The Basics."
3. Begin by cutting the largest heart from the fabric and webbing. Center it on the background and fuse it in place.
4. Cut the fabrics and webbing for the top and bottom of the middle-sized heart.
5. The center strip is made up of a 8" piece of 1" ribbon and ½" flat trim. Trace the center strip pattern piece on the webbing, cut it out, and place the two strips of ribbon over the pattern piece.
6. Place the middle-sized heart pieces and the center ribbon strip over the large heart as the pattern shows, and fuse.
7. Cut the small-sized center heart, and fuse it over the middle heart.
8. Lay the background fabric over two layers of Thermolam, and pin it in place. Machine quilt all the heart edges with invisible thread using a narrow zigzag stitch.
9. Glue the trims in place.
10. Follow the framing instructions in the section on "Framing and Finishing" to finish the picture.

Finished size: 11" x 14".

16. Bordered Fan

The Bordered Fan project uses four fans to create a bordered look. The use of black with pastels and the crisp white background suggests a feminine, almost old-fashioned look. The blocks just weren't complete without the added hand quilting. The picot-edged ribbon bows at the corners carry through on the theme. This is a special gift anytime for a person you want to remember. Wall quilts may not warm the toes, but they certainly warm the heart. This also makes a great friendship quilt.

Design runs the same size as the pattern shown. (Refer to pattern on page 69 and photo on page 38.)

MATERIALS

(Refer to Figure 22 for placement.)
¾ yd. of fabric for background and backing
⅛ yd. each of fabric for Pieces A, B, C, D, E, F, G, and H
fabric scrap for Piece I
6 yds. of ⅛" ribbon to outline fan designs and border
1½ yds. of ⅛" ribbon for edge of fan
1⅛ yds. of ⅛" ribbon for fan wedges
2⅔ yds. of 1/16" ribbon for border sections
1¼ yds. of ¼" flat lace for outer fan edge
½ yd. of ⅛" ribbon for bows
2 yds. of ⅜" picot-edged ribbon for outer bows
8 roses of two different colors for corners
20 small pearls that can be sewed on
1 yd. of paper-backed fusible webbing
⅝ yd. of Thermolam
invisible thread

INSTRUCTIONS

1. Cut out two pieces of background fabric and one piece of Thermolam, each 22" x 22". Fuse and cut out all of the pieces needed for the fans and borders. Read the general instructions on appliqué in "The Basics."
2. Place the pieces on the background fabric (see Figures 22 and 23), and fuse in place.
3. Glue all the trims in place.
4. Layer the quilt, and pin it together. Use invisible thread and a narrow zigzag stitch; stitch on the inner and outer border ribbons, and then on the fan section divisions and top edge of the fan.
5. Trim excess fabric so quilt measures 21" x 21". Hand quilt around the edges of the fans and the border. See Figure 24.

6. Bind the quilt, following the general instructions in the section on "Borders and Bindings."
7. Hand tack the pearls, ribbon roses, and corner bows in place.

Finished size: 21" x 21".

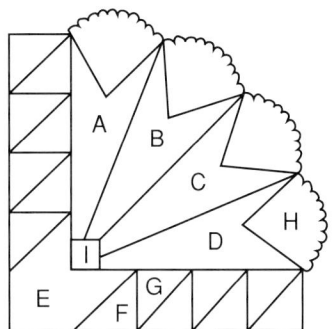

FIG. 22

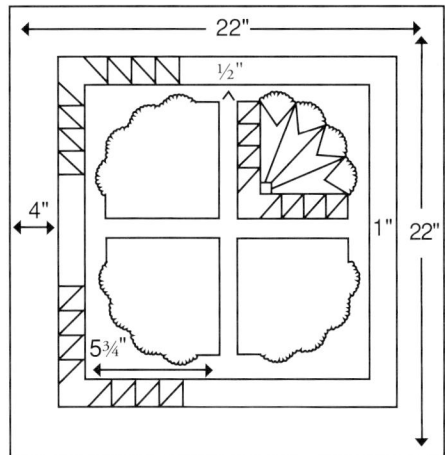

FIG. 23

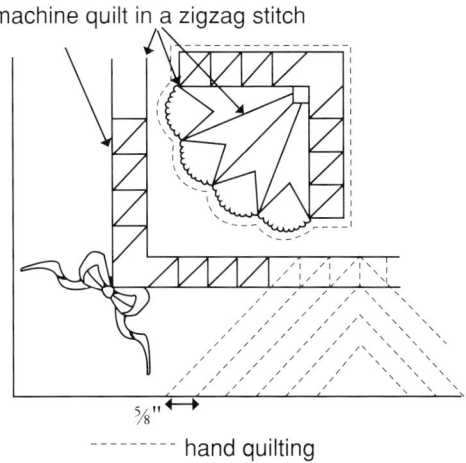

FIG. 24

17. Bunny Kisses Quilt

Two bunnies snuggle up to hold a pieced heart in this quilt design. The hearts are then repeated in three borders to give a fresh new appeal to this child's quilt. The designs are all machine appliquéd, and then machine quilted. This could be hung on the wall or placed in the crib to keep baby warm. The bunny design can be put on other projects, as well, as you will see. Our bunny quilt has a definite feminine feeling, but that can be changed by varying the color choices.

Design runs the same size as the pattern shown. (Refer to pattern on page 68 and photo on page 39.)

Materials

1⅜ yds. of background fabric
¼ yd. of fabric for bunnies
1⅝ yds. of fabric for hearts and back of quilt
½ yd. of fabric for middle heart and binding
¼ yd. of fabric for bottom heart
⅛ yd. of fabric for connecting square
⅞ yd. of ⅜" ribbon for bows
1⅜ yds. of bonded batting
1¼ yds. of paper-backed fusible webbing
1 yd. of tear-away stabilizer for appliqué
matching thread for all appliqué fabrics
invisible thread for machine quilting

Instructions

1. Cut the background fabric, backing, and batting, each piece measuring 32" x 46".
2. Cut the two bunnies out of the fusible webbing, reversing one of them so they will face each other. Fuse the webbing to the wrong side of the bunny fabric. Cut out the bunny shapes. Read the general instructions on fusing and trimming in "The Basics."
3. To make the hearts, cut three strips each of the top, middle, and bottom fabrics:
   3 of the top, each 1¾" x 44"
   3 of the middle, each 1½" x 44"
   3 of the bottom, each 2½" x 44"
Stitch the strips together using a ¼" seam allowance. Press the seams in one direction (Figure 25).

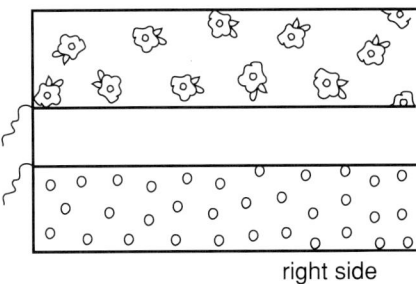

right side

FIG. 25

4. Cut out 19 heart shapes from the fusible webbing. Fuse the shapes to the wrong side of the stripped fabric (Figure 26). Cut out the hearts.

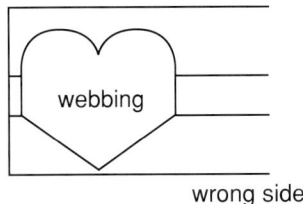

FIG. 26

5. Cut out 15 connecting squares from fusible webbing. Fuse them to the wrong side of the fabric, and cut out.
6. Starting at the bottom of the background fabric, measure up 9". Mark this line across the fabric by lightly pressing it. Center six heart shapes ¾" apart across the fabric. Fuse in place. Add five connecting squares between the hearts. Fuse in place.
7. Repeat this heart row two more times 6½" apart, coming up the quilt (Figure 27).
8. Center the bunnies 1½" above the top of the hearts with their paws 1" apart. Position the remaining heart between the bunnies. Fuse in place.
9. Cut tear-away stabilizer to fit behind the bunnies and heart. Pin on the back of the fabric. Machine appliqué. Change the thread color with any change of fabric in the appliqué.
10. Cut tear-away stabilizer for each row of hearts until the hearts are all appliquéd.
11. Layer the quilt by placing the backing down first, wrong side up. Then add the batting, and then the top, right-side up. Put layers together by pinning about every 6".

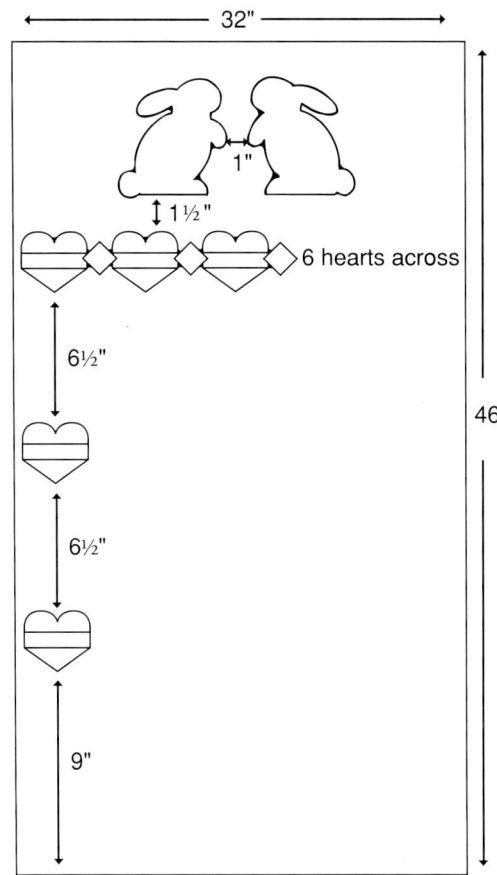

FIG. 27

12. Machine quilt around the edges of the bunnies and hearts using invisible thread on the top and regular thread on the bottom. Use the presser foot as the guide so the stitching is about ¼" away from the appliqués (Figure 28).
13. Cut four strips of binding, each 1½" wide by 44". Sew all the strips together. Follow the binding instructions in the section on "Borders and Bindings."

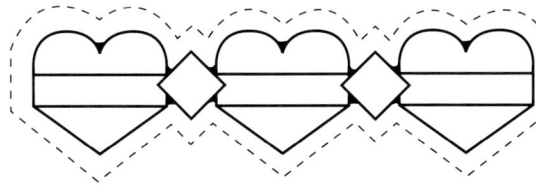

FIG. 28

Finished size: 32" x 46".

18. Bunny Kisses Pillow

This is a great Easter giveable. By varying the heart placement, you'll make bunny seem to be rolling a heart-shaped egg. This also makes a sweet pillow that could please anyone from a baby to a teen.

Design runs the same size as the pattern shown. (Refer to pattern on page 68 and photo on page 39.)

MATERIALS
- ½ yd. of fabric for background and backing
- ⅓ yd. of fabric for ruffle
- ¼ yd. of fabric for bunny
- three 2" x 5" fabrics for the heart
- ½ yd. of ¼" ribbon for bow
- ¼ yd. of ½" ribbon for heart
- ¼ yd. of ⅜" flat trim for heart
- small pearl bead for eye
- small heart cut from heart trim for nose
- ½ yd. of Thermolam
- ¼ yd. of paper-backed fusible webbing
- invisible thread
- 12 oz. of Polyfil pillow stuffing

INSTRUCTIONS
1. Cut background fabric, backing, and Thermolam, each piece measuring 16" x 16".
2. For added dimension to the bunny and heart, Thermolam was fused to each. Then they are fused to the background. Read the general instructions on fusing and trimming in "The Basics."
3. The heart is tilted instead of being positioned as it is shown on the pattern, to give it more of an egg look. To make the heart, add ¼" seam allowance on the interior seams. Then machine stitch the sections together before cutting out the heart. Now it can be fused in place.
4. After the fusing is finished, all trims, ribbons, nose, and eye are sewn on.
5. Pin the pillow top to the Thermolam. Machine quilt around the edges of the design using a tiny zigzag stitch and invisible thread.
6. Cut three pieces of fabric, each 3¾" wide and 44" long, for the ruffle. Stitch the three pieces together lengthwise, making a circle. Hem one edge by turning it under ¼", then turn it a second time, and stitch. Run a basting line of stitching ¼" away from the edge. Pull up the bobbin thread to gather the ruffle. Arrange the fullness evenly around the edge of the pillow. Pin ruffle in place and stitch to the top of the pillow.
7. Finish pillow construction following the instructions in the section on "Pillows."

Finished size: 15" x 15", plus a 3" ruffle on all sides.

19. Bears and Bow Ties Quilt

Just recently a good friend and former babysitter of my (Jean's) almost-grown children had her first baby, a boy. I just wanted to make something very special for Ethan. A big boy quilt for when he moves into his first bed was the idea. His daddy is a contractor so I felt the plaid-shirt look would be especially sweet. Making a gift for someone you know gives you the opportunity to specialize. Plaids abound on the teddy bears as well as around the border on this quilt.

Design runs the same size as the pattern shown. (Refer to pattern on pages 70-71 and photo on page 40.)

Materials

(Refer to Figure 30 for yardage placement.)
1¼ yds. of background fabric
¾ yd. of fabric for bears
¼ yd. each of six plaid fabrics for shirts and grid
½ yd. of fabric for first border and binding
¾ yd. of fabric for second border
1⅝ yds. of backing fabric
1⅝ yds. of 3 oz. bonded quilt batting
1½ yds. of paper-backed fusible webbing
1½ yds. of tear-away stabilizer for appliqué
thread for appliquéing bears
invisible thread for quilting
six-strand black embroidery floss for face

Instructions

1. Cut four pieces of background fabric, each measuring 10½" x 30½". Cut three strips of the six plaid fabrics, 1½" x 44" each. From the paper-backed fusible webbing, cut out 11 bears and 11 shirts.
2. Fuse the webbing to the bears and plaid shirts. Read the general instructions on fusing and trimming in "The Basics." Fuse the shirts to the bears.
3. Position the bears on the background fabric according to Figure 30. Fuse them in place.
4. Machine appliqué.
5. Lightly mark the face with a lead pencil. Use three strands of embroidery floss, and outline the nose and mouth. Make a French knot for the eyes (Figure 32).
6. To make bow ties, use the leftover 1½" squares from the border. Fold a square in half with the raw edges touching in the middle of the bow. Pin. With needle and thread, gather the bow tightly in the middle. Hand stitch to the shirts.
7. Lay out the plaid strips in the order you want. Stitch them together using a ¼" seam allowance. (The strips will be repeated three times.) Press seam allowances in one direction.
8. Cut across the strips 1½" wide (Figure 31).
9. Stitch these pieces into one very long strip.
10. Stitch the strips between the rows of the background fabric. There will be 30 squares in each row. There are two rows between each background panel. (Just count out 30 and tear apart the stitching.)
11. Add a strip of 46 squares to each side and 32 squares to the top and bottom.
12. Cut five strips for the first border, each 1" x 45". Stitch these into one long strip. Sew a border strip to each side of the quilt. Sew border strips to the top and bottom.
13. Cut five strips for the second border, each 2½" x 45". Stitch as in instruction #11.
14. Cut backing and batting. Layer the quilt, and pin it together for quilting. Machine quilt with invisible thread on the top, as seen in Figure 29. For more instructions on machine quilting, read the section on "Quilting."
15. The binding for the quilt is the same fabric as the first border. Cut five strips, each 1½" x 45". Add the binding strips as you did for the borders. Hand stitch in place to the backing.

Finished size: 37" x 53".

FIG. 29

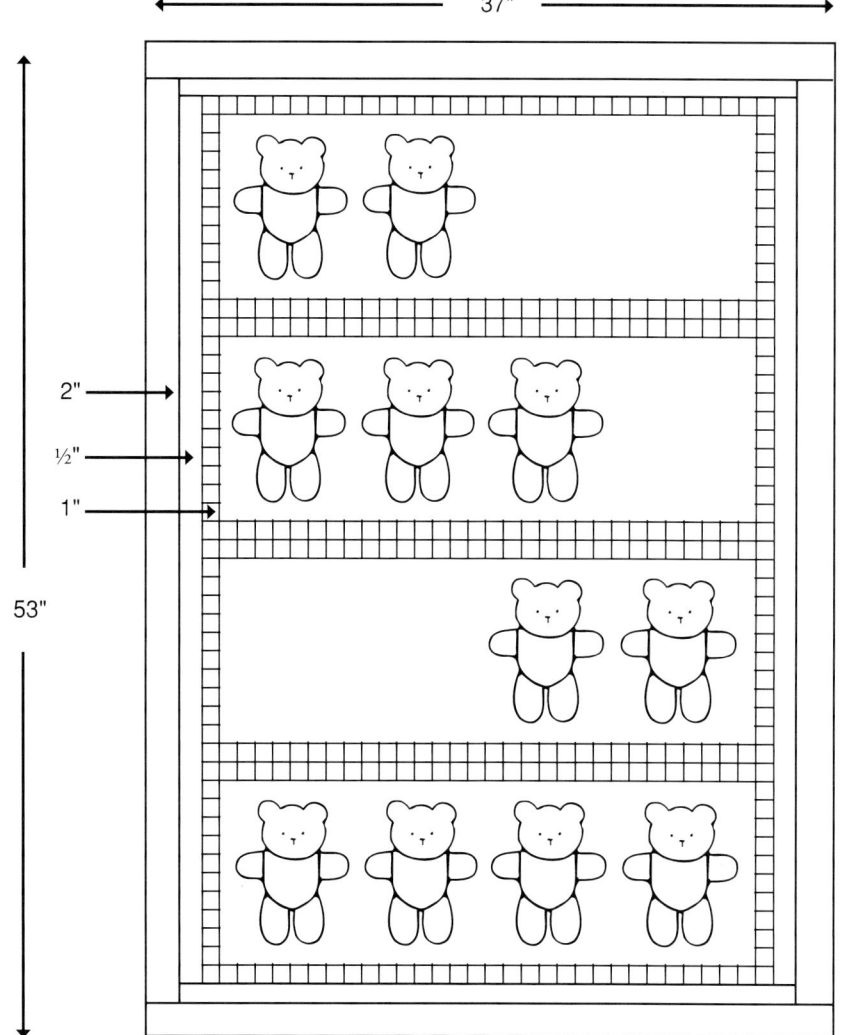

FIG. 30

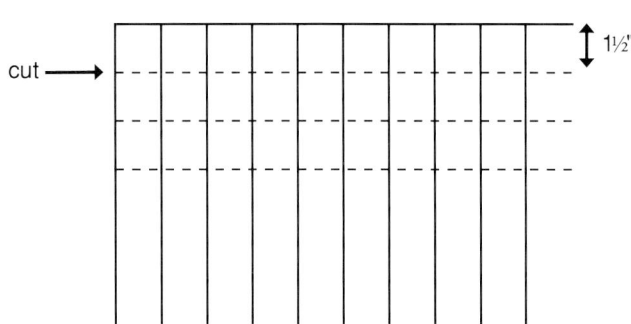

FIG. 31

FIG. 32

20. Bears and Bow Ties Nap Pillow

The idea for this pillow was prompted because I (Marina) am one of many working mothers. Scotty, my four-year-old, needed a pillow for naptime at his pre-school. I felt the best way for both of us to feel better about time spent apart was to send a little stitched and stuffed "love" with him to school.

Design runs the same size as the pattern shown. (Refer to pattern on pages 70-71 and photo on page 40.)

MATERIALS

(Refer to Figure 33 for fabric placement.)
½ yd. of fabric for Piece A and for backing
⅛ yd. of fabric for Piece B and bow tie
⅛ yd. of fabric for Piece C
1 yd. of ⅜" grosgrain ribbon for Piece D
¼ yd. of fabric for Piece E
58" of piping for edge
7" x 9" of fabric for bear body
3½" x 3½" of fabric for shirt
⅔ yd. of Thermolam for bear and pillow top
¼ yd. of paper-backed fusible webbing
black embroidery floss
invisible thread
12 oz. pillow stuffing

INSTRUCTIONS

1. Cut out the following pieces, referring to Figure 33 and the pattern.
    bear out of fabric, webbing, and Thermolam
    bear shirt out of fabric and webbing
    for Piece A, cut 1 piece, 10¼" x 10¼"
    for Piece B, cut 4 pieces, each 1" x 11"
    for Piece C, cut 2 squares, each 3½" x 3½"
        (then cut across the squares diagonally to make the triangles)
    for Piece D, cut 4 lengths of ribbon, each 8"
    for Piece E, cut 2 squares, each 6¾" x 6¾"
        (cut diagonally)
    for Piece F, cut piping 58" long
    Cut pillow back and Thermolam, each 14½" x 14½". Read the general instructions on fusing, dimensional fusing, and trimming in the chapter on "The Basics."
2. Fuse the fabric bear to the Thermolam, then fuse the bear and Thermolam to Piece A.
3. Fuse the shirt in place. Mark the face lightly with pencil.
4. To make bow tie for the bear, follow instruction #6 in the Bears and Bow Ties Quilt project (page 45).

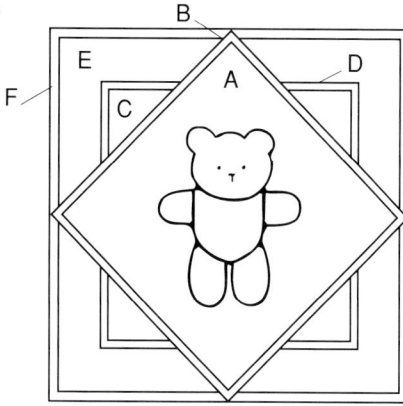

FIG. 33

5. Place Piece C on E, butting the diagonal raw edges together (Figure 34). Place the 8" length of ribbon over the raw edge of Piece C. Pin. As you come to the corner, tuck the ribbon under so it makes a square corner. Top-stitch the ribbon in place. Repeat on all four corners.

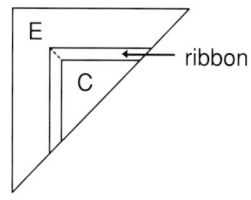

FIG. 34

6. Using a ¼" seam allowance, add B pieces to each side of Piece A. Press.
7. Add the E pieces, using a ¼" seam allowance. Press.
8. Layer the pillow top on Thermolam. Pin in place. Machine zigzag with invisible thread around the bear and shirt shape.
9. For the eyes, make a French knot (Figure 32). Use three strands of floss to outline the nose and mouth.
10. Place the raw edge of the piping on the raw edge of the pillow. Pin in place. Where the two raw edge ends meet, overlap them so the raw edges will be inside of the pillow.
11. Use a zipper foot and stitch around the edge of the piping on the stitching line.
12. To finish the pillow, follow the general instructions in the section on "Pillows."

Finished size: 14" x 14".

21. Star Bright

Enter into the galaxy of starry nights with this wall-hanging, featured on the cover. Floral fabrics combine with a paisley and prints in the pieced stars. Star sequins, pearls, and simple quilt stitches with metallic thread add to the "out of this world" effect.

Design runs the same size as the pattern shown. (Refer to pattern on pages 71-72 and photo on cover.)

Materials

- ⅞ yd. of background fabric
- ⅛ yd. of seven different fabrics for stars
- 5" x 5" lamé for center star
- 1½ yds. of ⅛" cord for center streamers
- 1½ yds. of ¹⁄₁₆" ribbon for center streamers
- ½ yd. each of two ⅜" ribbons for stars
- ½ yd. each of three other ⅛" ribbons for stars
- ½ yd. of narrow lace for stars
- 4 yds. of ⅛" ribbon to edge stars
- 20 pearls, each ¼"
- 30 beads, each ⅛"
- package of star sequins
- ¾ yd. of paper-backed fusible webbing
- silver quilting thread
- ⅞ yd. of Thermolam

Instructions

1. Cut the background fabric to a piece that measures 25" x 28". Cut the Thermolam the same size.
2. Fold the fabric in quarters and gently press in the creases. Open up the fabric. When this project is completed, one star will appear in each of the sections (Figure 35), positioned 2" from the center fold and 2" from the cross fold. Our stars are a mirror image of each other. To achieve that, trace the star on the back of the tracing paper. Trace two stars from one side of the paper on to the paper-backed fusible webbing. Now trace the other two stars from the back side of the tracing paper. This gives a mirror image of the stars.
3. Follow the general instructions for appliqué and application of trims from the chapter on "The Basics."
4. Follow the instructions on construction in "The Basics" for adding the streamers that come out from the stars.
5. Once the trims are glued in place, put the star picture on top of the Thermolam. Mark the quilting lines. Pin the two layers together, then add the quilting lines.
6. Frame the picture.

Finished size: 23" x 26".

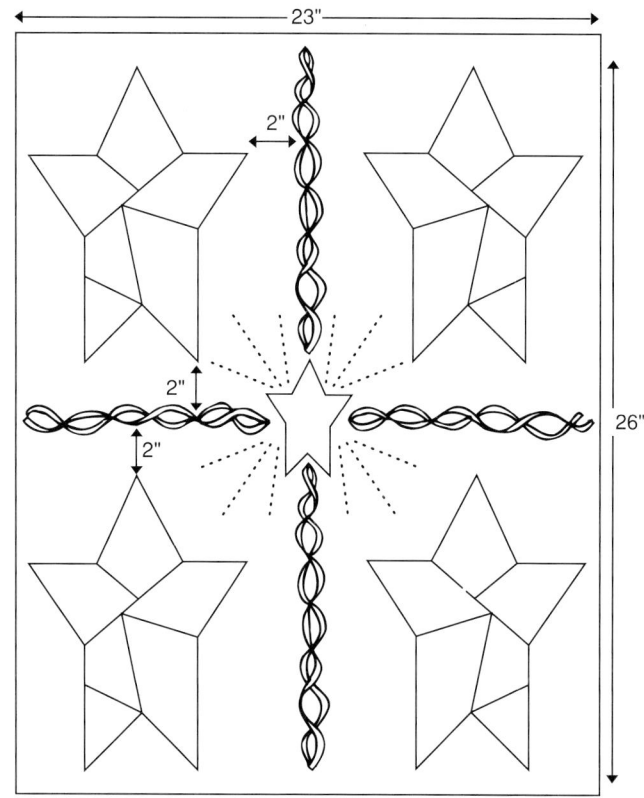

FIG. 35

Wrapping It Up

Paper, ribbon, tissue, and a bow....wrapping a gift is an important finale. Following through on a handwork theme, we have included gift tag designs to complement your package.

Again we suggest you utilize your local copy shop in reproducing these tag designs. The tags are inexpensive and easy, yet will add a special, personal touch to your "gift of heart and hand." The paper best suited (weightwise) for this is cover stock. There are a multitude of colors to choose from, though a simple white is always appropriate. Embossing ink and powder add an elegant sparkle of interest, or you can borrow the felt pens from the kids and color away!

Another gifty idea is wrapping your picture in some yardage used in your design. Ribbons and trims used can also be added in the bow. They also give the new beginnings for another project.

Remember that these designs have applications for many projects. Let the copy machine be your friend in enlarging and reducing designs. Let your creative juices flow!

*It has been a special treat for us to share **Picture This** with you. We hope that through example and word, we have sparked that urge to create, motivating the "gift of heart" through a "gift of hand."*

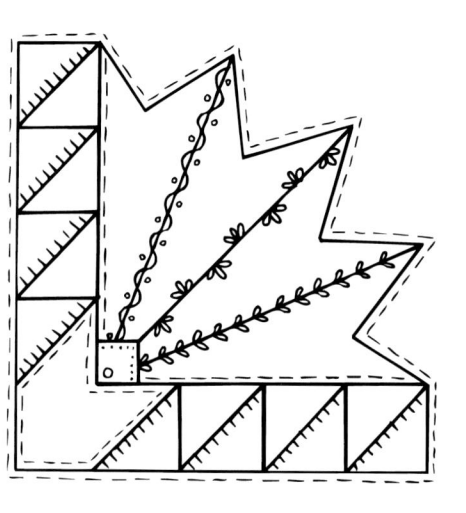

Gift Tags

About the Authors

Jean Wells and Marina Anderson have been working together creatively since they met at The Stitchin' Post in Sisters, Oregon, twelve years ago. Jean had recently opened her quilt shop and Marina dropped in full of ideas. A relationship of heart and hand developed immediately. Not only has Marina been responsible for the art work for the store over the years, but she has also illustrated most of Jean's publications, including *Patchworthy Apparel*, *Vesting*, and *Fans*.

A Celebration of Hearts, jointly written by Jean and Marina, was published in 1988 by C&T Publishing. By joining their unique talents, the authors have contributed innovative ideas to the growing quilting and craft industry. Both authors are freelance designers working out of their homes. Jean also operates her quilt shop and participates in the lecture circuit.

Jean Wells: Sewing, embroidery, and quilting have been a part of Jean's life for as long as she can remember. Trained as a home economist and counselor, she taught home economics for several years before starting her own business. For the past fifteen years, Jean has built her own niche in the quilting design world as an author, shop owner, teacher, and designer. Her designs are seen in Leisure Arts books, McCall's Patterns, Good Housekeeping, Family Circle, Quilting USA, and Creative Quilting. Offray Ribbons, Inc., Fabric Traditions, and Concord Fabrics keep her busy stitching up one-of-a-kind creations for their showrooms.

Jean's children are almost grown. Jason, 21, is in the army and Valori, 17, is an aspiring graphic artist. Husband John is a very supportive partner in her endeavors. She still finds time to serve on boards of directors for economic development, state small business management programs, and national quilt market. Occasionally she even gardens and plays golf.

Marina Anderson: Marina has illustrated and designed for the fabric arts field for many years. Finding that special way to put on paper or to create in fabric and wood what we all find at the heart level has always been her main objective. You may find more of her work in cross-stitch and appliqué books by Leisure Arts, cross-stitch designs in books by Vanessa Ann, projects for children by Oxmoor House, and possibly even a coloring page brought home by your child—Marina also illustrates educational publications. Her most recent artistic endeavors will be seen soon in the Daisy Kingdom product line.

Marina and husband Jeff recently moved to the mountain community of Bend, Oregon. Their family includes Danya (14), who loves to dabble in fabric, Nicholas (10), a budding artist, and Scotty (5), who keeps the entire family in stitches.

PATTERNS

The Friendship Fan
(Instructions on page 19)

Oriental Fan
(Instructions on page 25)

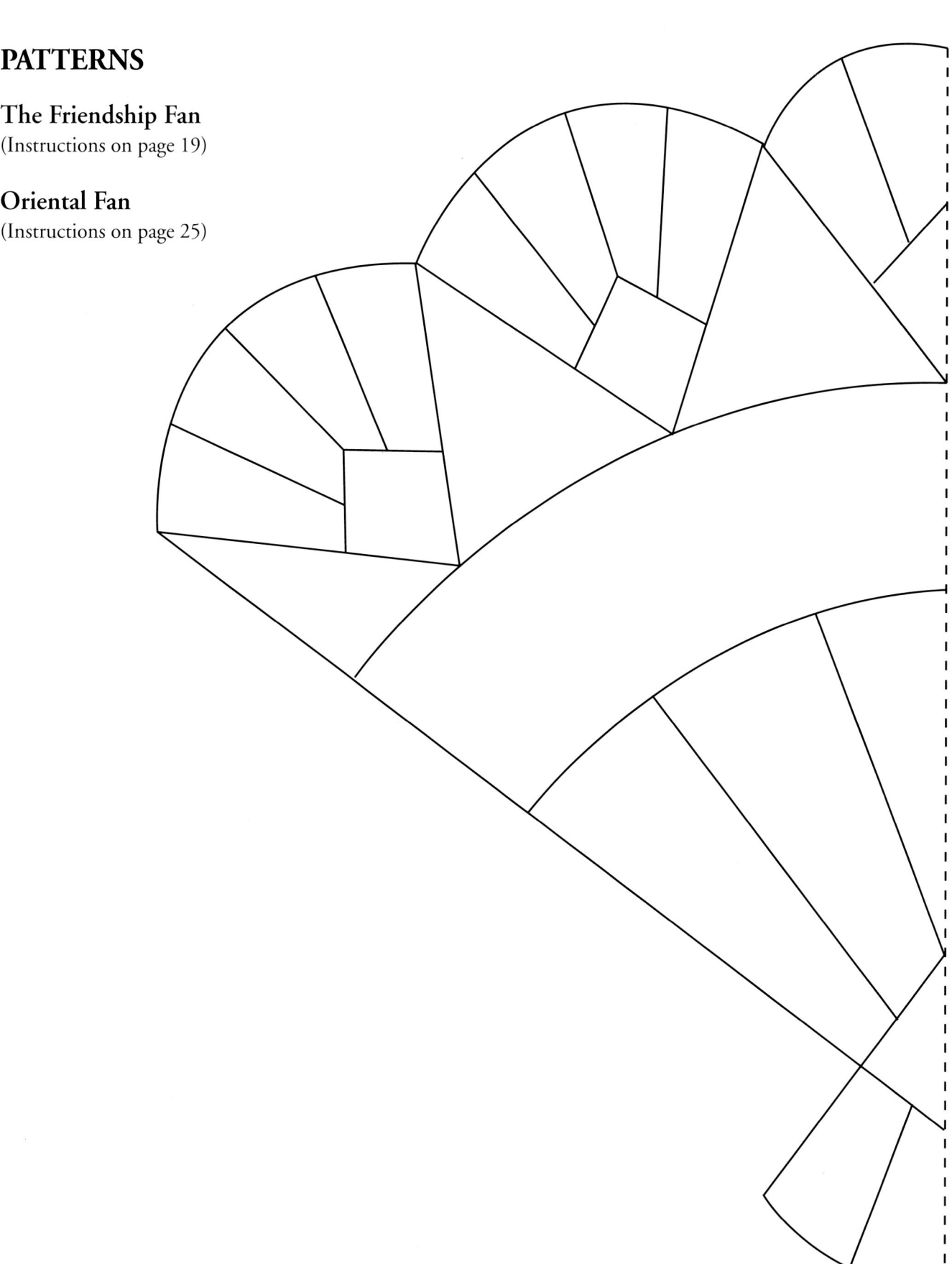

Quilter's Garden
Use dotted line. (Instructions on page 20)

Evening Quilter's Garden
Use dotted triangle. (Instructions on page 20)

Patterns 53

Crazy Patch Heart
(Instructions on page 25)

Corner Fan
(Instructions on page 29)

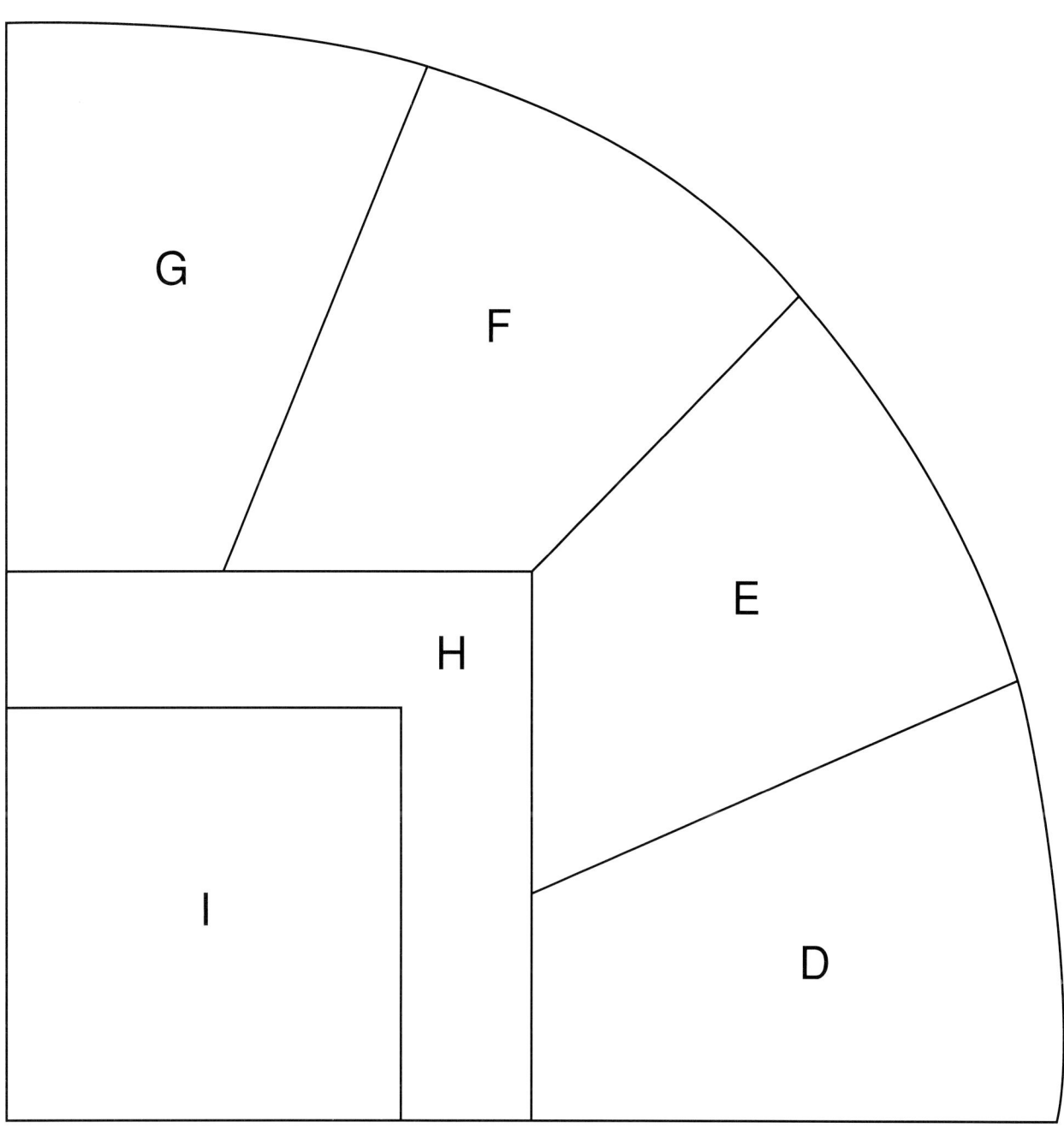

Patterns 55

Heavenly Angel
1 of 4 pages
(Instructions on page 26)

Celestial Angel
1 of 4 pages
(Instructions on page 28)

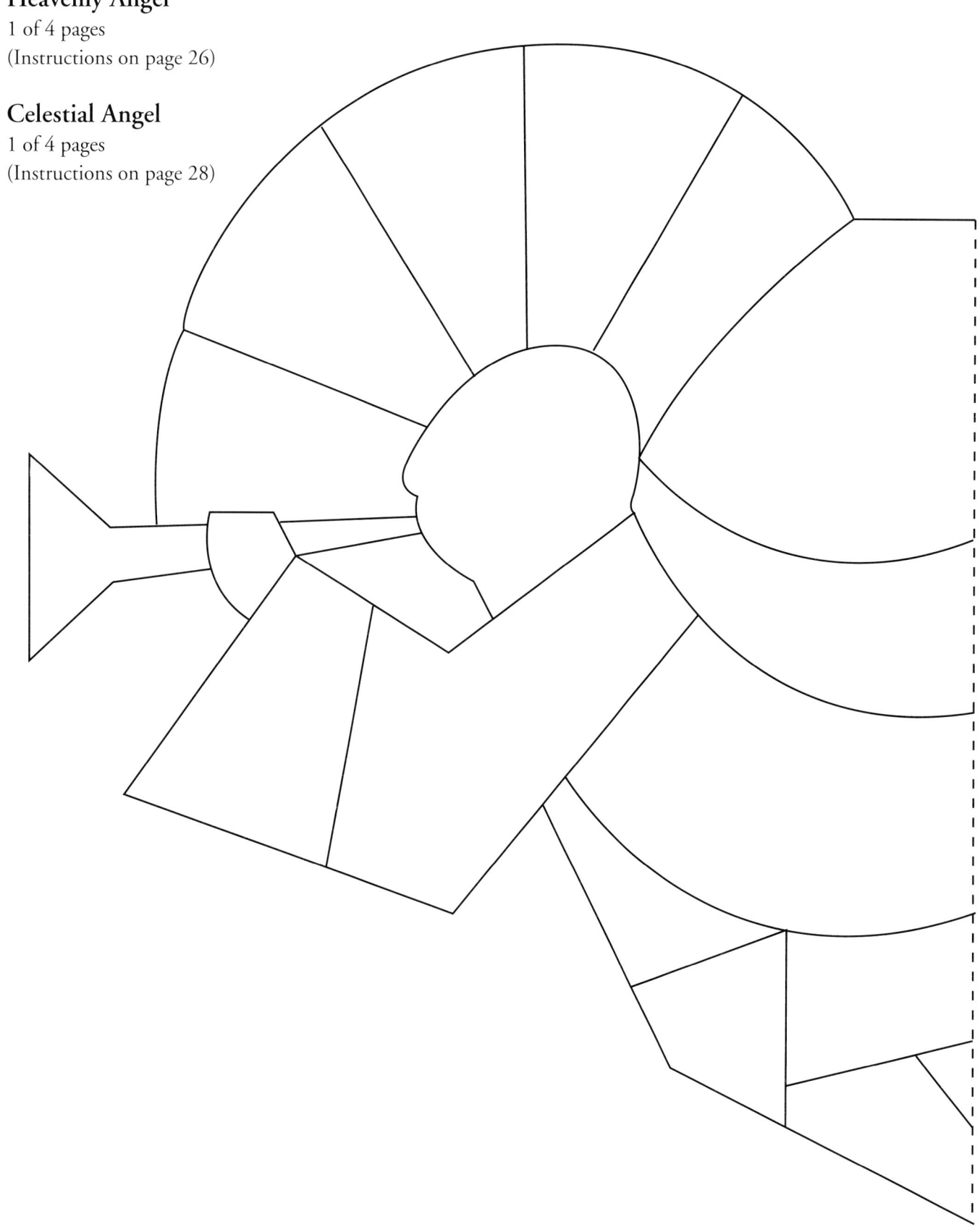

Heavenly Angel
2 of 4 pages
(Instructions on page 26)

Celestial Angel
2 of 4 pages
(Instructions on page 28)

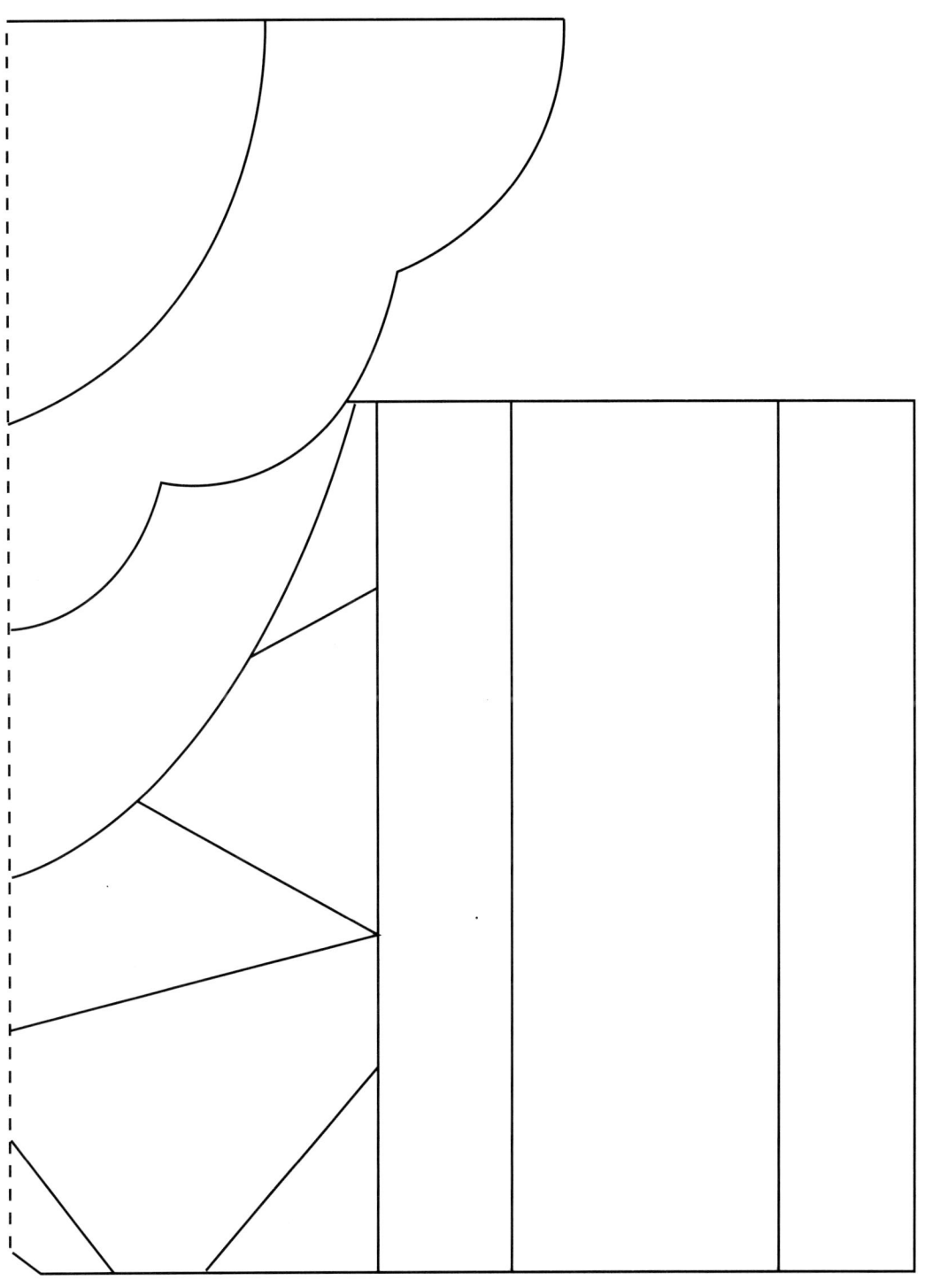

Heavenly Angel
3 of 4 pages
(Instructions on page 26)

Celestial Angel
3 of 4 pages
(Instructions on page 28)

A

A

Heavenly Angel
4 of 4 pages
(Instructions on page 26)

Celestial Angel
4 of 4 pages
(Instructions on page 28)

Old-fashioned Santa
1 of 2 pages
(Instructions on page 27)

Victorian Santa
1 of 2 pages
(Instructions on page 31)

Old-fashioned Santa
2 of 2 pages
(Instructions on page 27)

Victorian Santa
2 of 2 pages
(Instructions on page 31)

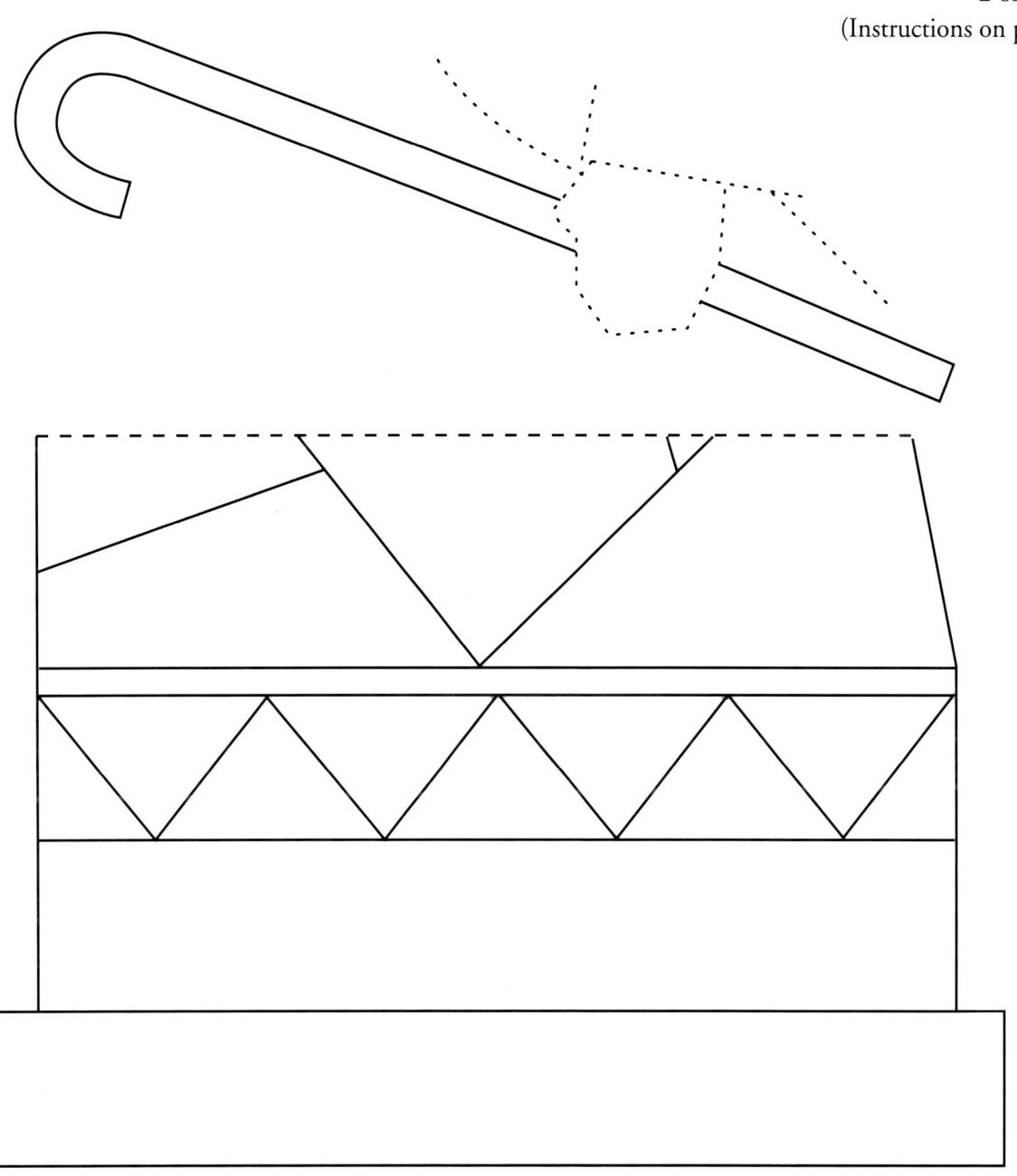

Christmas Tree
1 of 2 pages
(Instructions on pages 27-28)

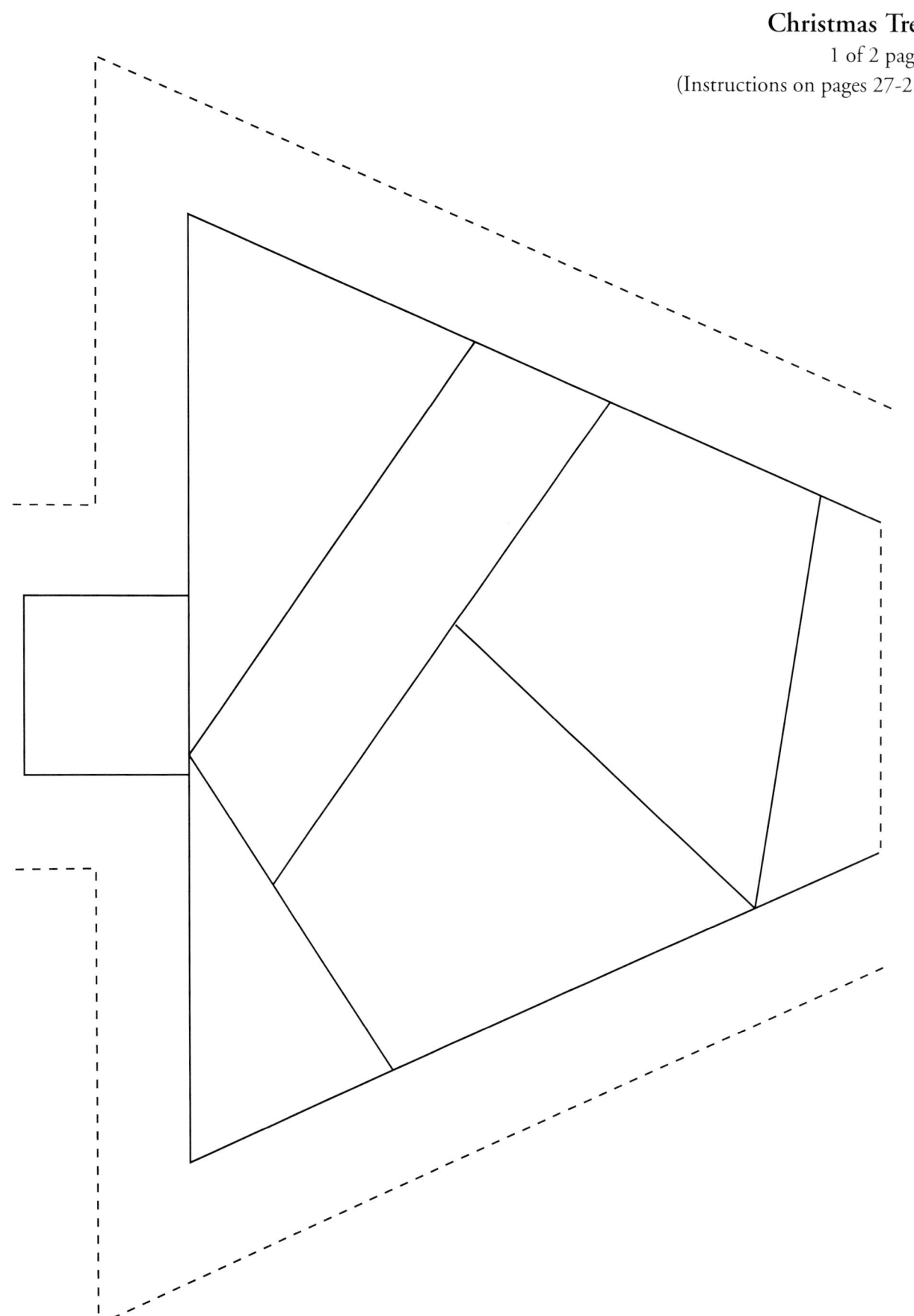

Christmas Tree
2 of 2 pages
(Instructions on pages 27-28)

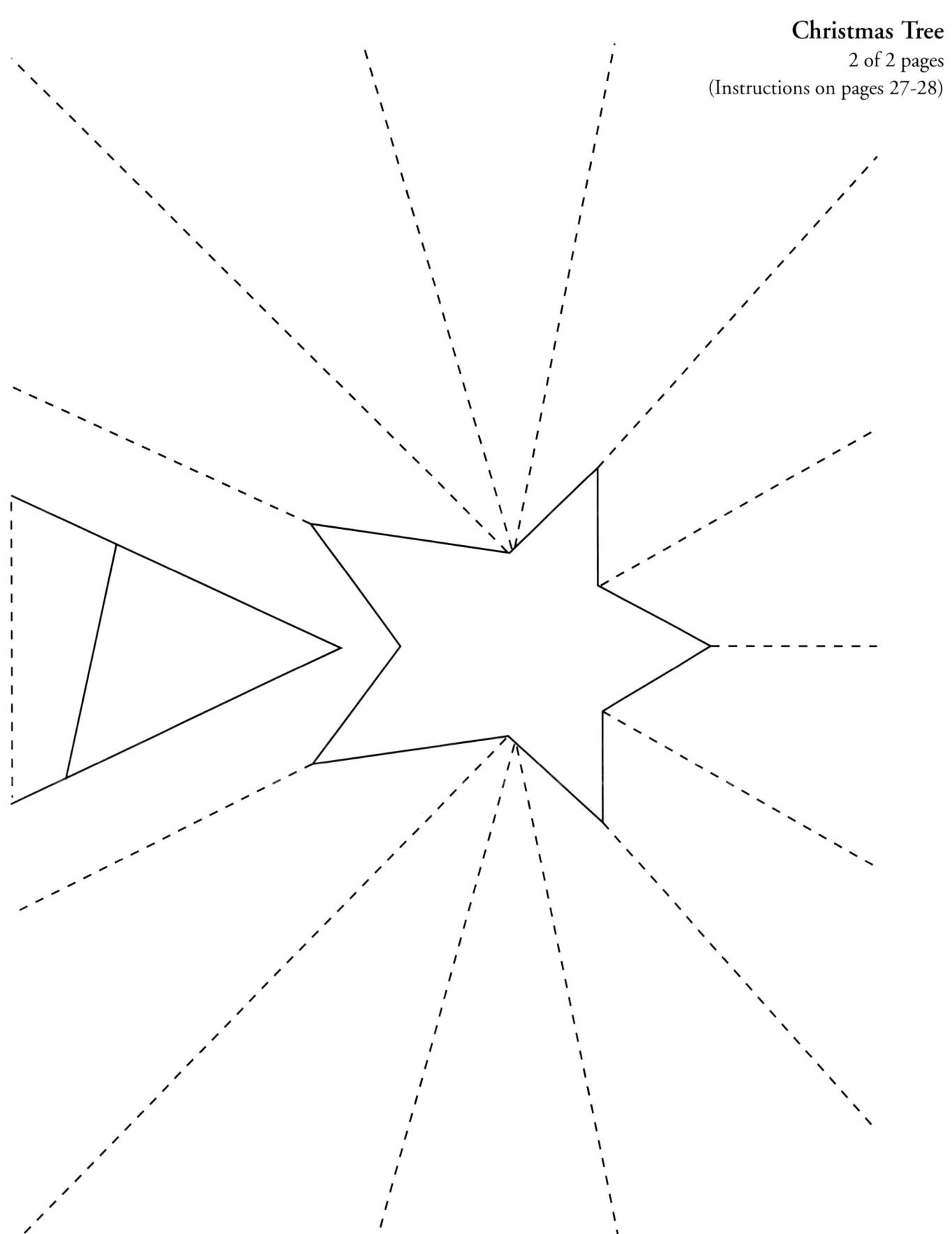

Pastel House and Heart
1 of 2 pages
(Instructions on page 30)

Country House and Heart
1 of 2 pages
(Instructions on page 31)

Pastel House and Heart
2 of 2 pages
(Instructions on page 30)

Country House and Heart
2 of 2 pages
(Instructions on page 31)

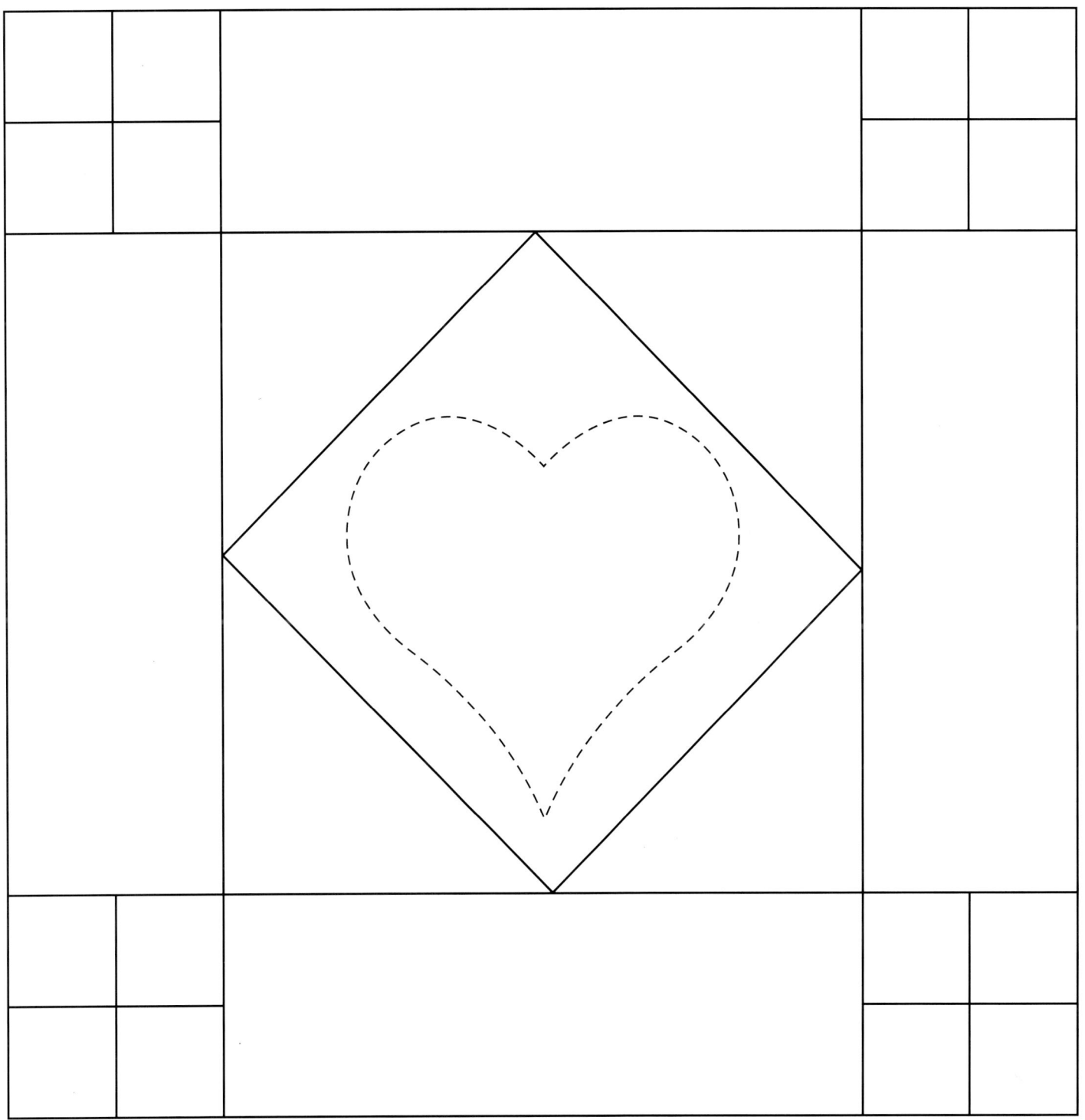

Tulip Fan

(Instructions on page 30)

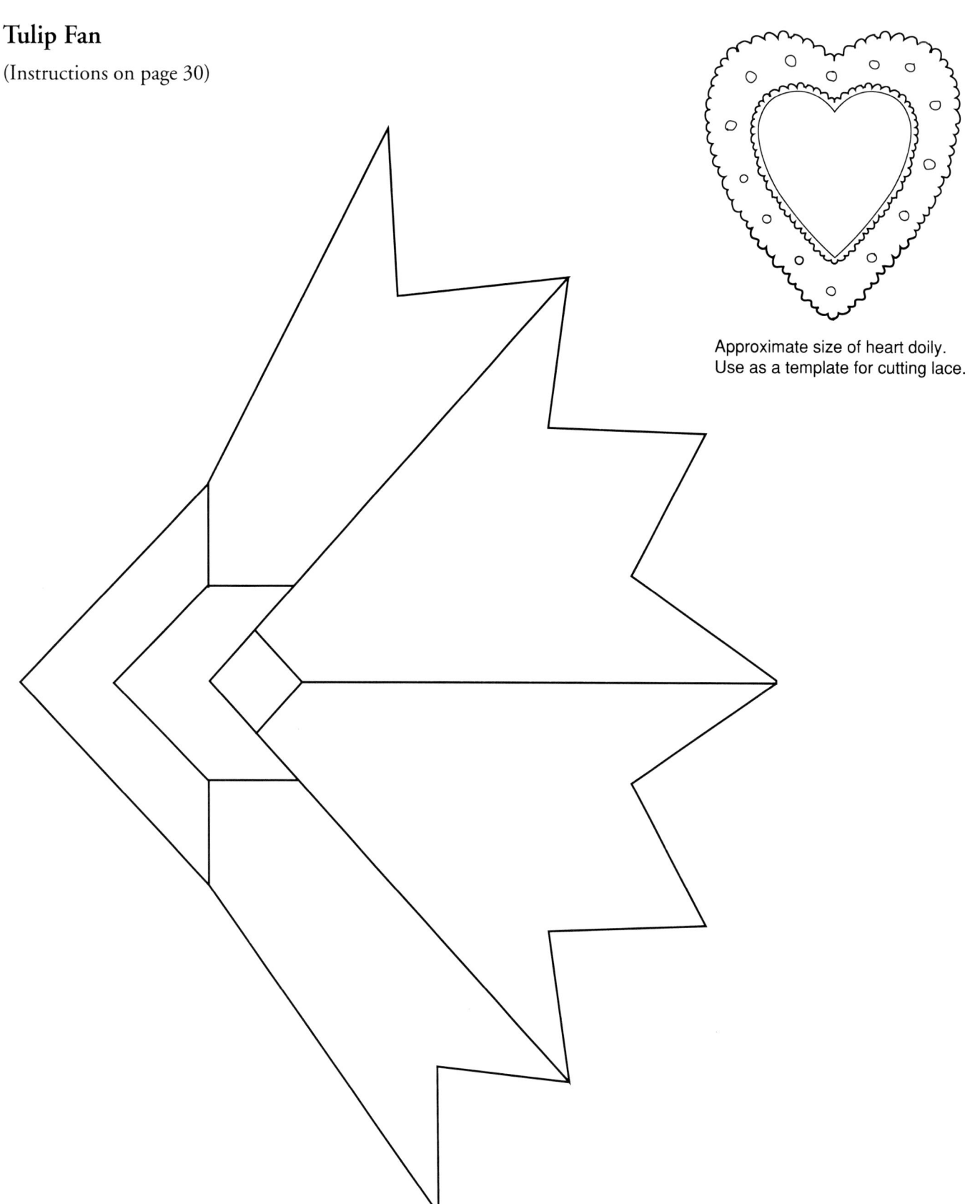

Approximate size of heart doily.
Use as a template for cutting lace.

Layered Hearts: Wedding Heart and Valentine Heart
(Instructions on pages 32 and 41)

Patterns 67

Bunny Kisses Quilt
(Instructions on pages 42-43)

Bunny Kisses Pillow
(Instructions on page 44)

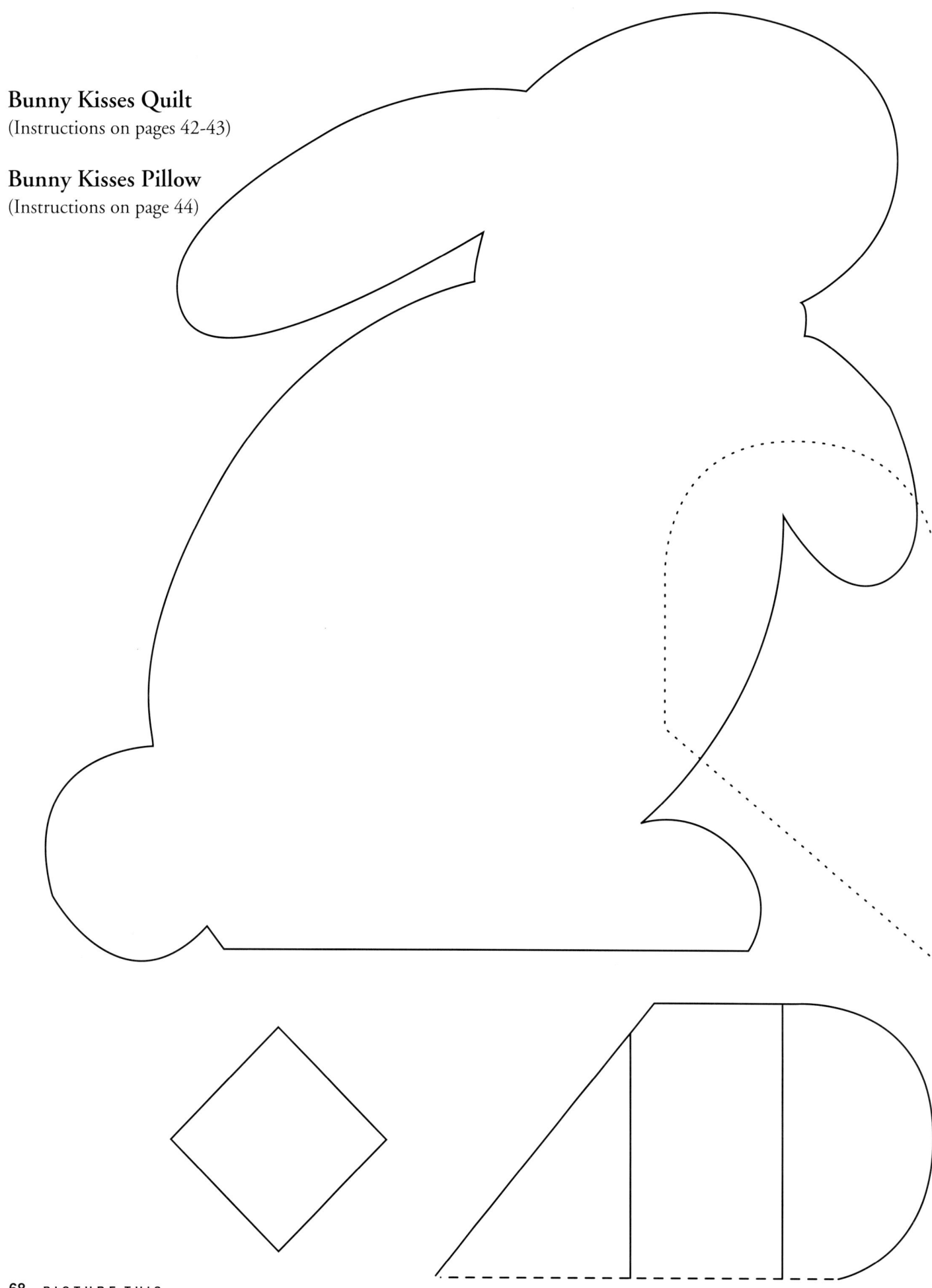

Bordered Fan

(Instructions on pages 41-42)

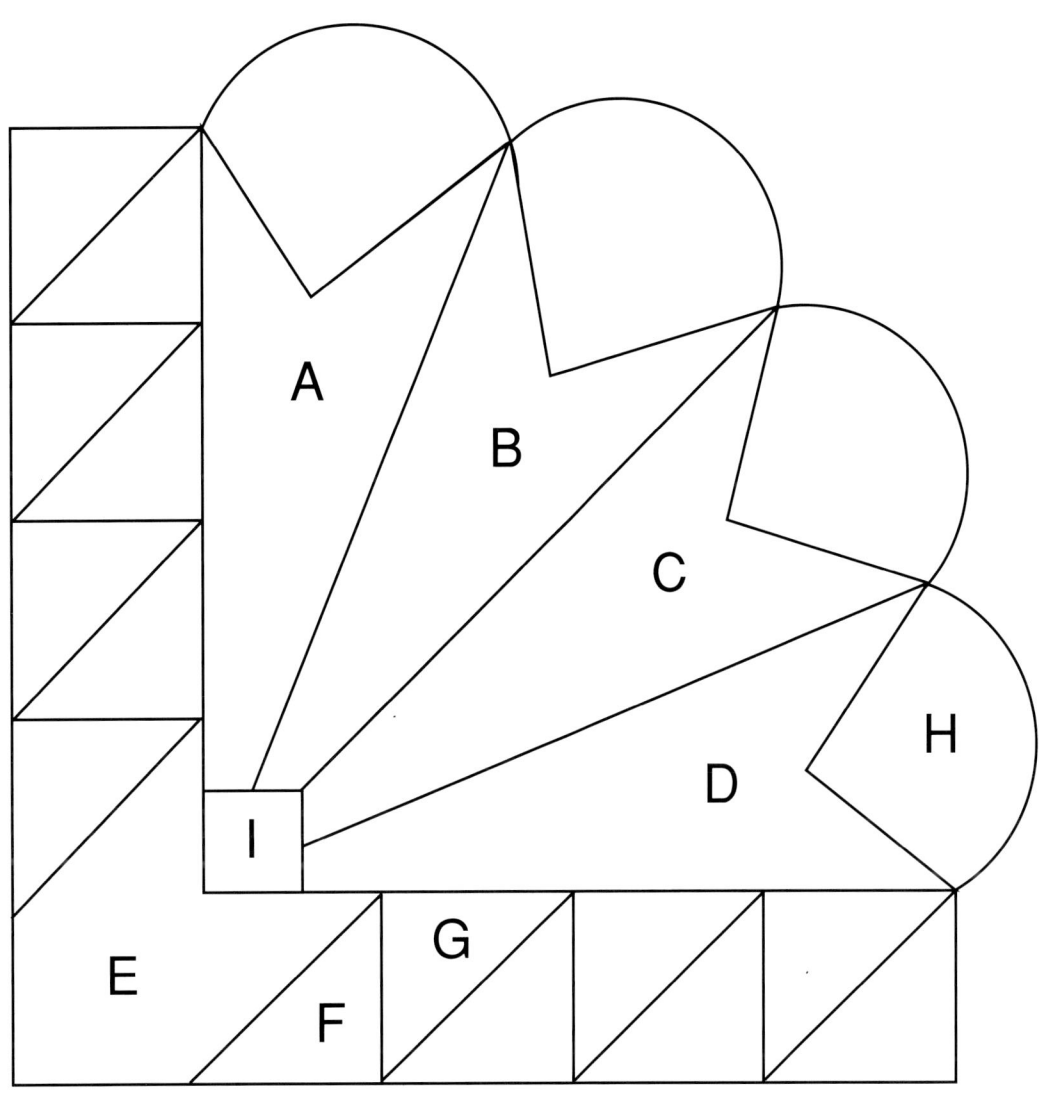

Patterns 69

Bears and Bow Ties Quilt
1 of 2 pages
(Instructions on pages 45-46)

Bears and Bow Ties Nap Pillow
1 of 2 pages
(Instructions on page 47)

Bears and Bow Ties Quilt
2 of 2 pages
(Instructions on pages 45-46)

Bears and Bow Ties Nap Pillow
2 of 2 pages
(Instructions on page 47)

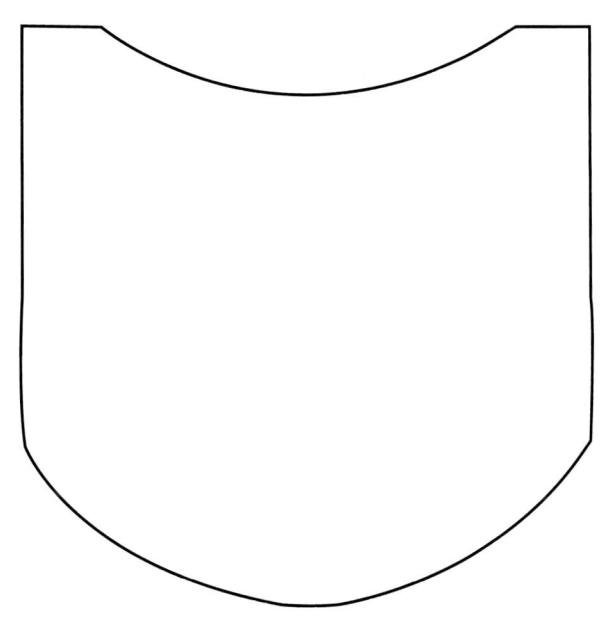

Star Bright
1 of 2 pages
(Instructions on page 48)

Star Bright
2 of 2 pages
(Instructions on page 48)

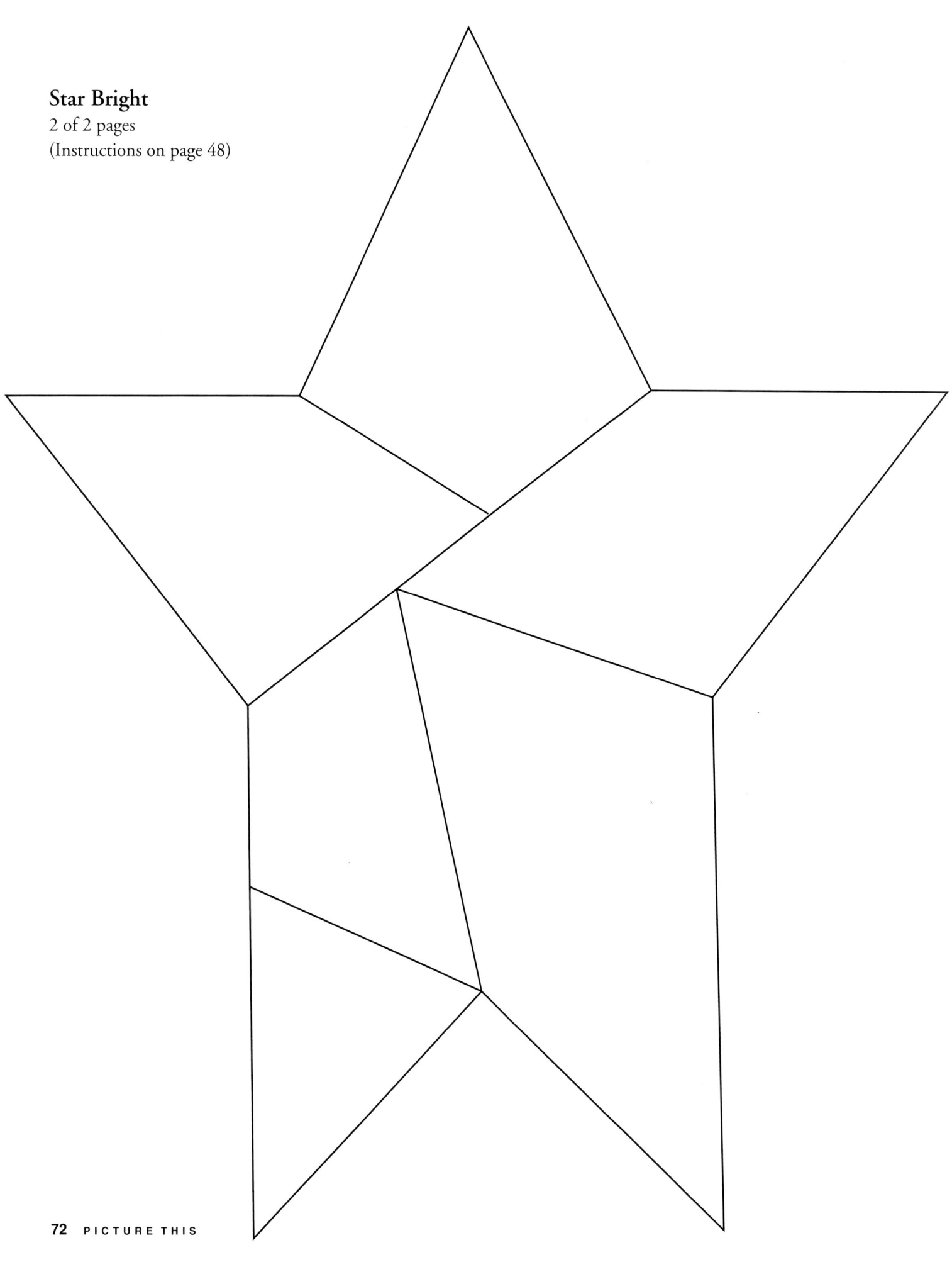